I0794678

THE RADICAL RESCUE

KIRSTEN A. ROGGENKAMP
AND HEATHER BLAIRE

Pacific Press®
Publishing Association
Nampa, Idaho | www.pacificpress.com

Cover design: Emily Bowen
Cover illustration: Lars Justinen/Goodsalt.com
Interior design: Aaron Troia

You can obtain additional copies of this book by calling toll-free 1-800-765-6955 or by visiting http://www.adventistbookcenter.com.

ISBN 978-0-8163-6810-5

December 2021

DEDICATION

With grateful hearts we dedicate
this book to the glory and honor of
Jesus Christ, the Radical Rescuer.

CONTENTS

Acknowledgments 7

Introduction 9

Part I—The Rescue Work Begins

Chapter 1: Radical Rescue Understood 13

Chapter 2: Hope for Tomorrow 19

Chapter 3: The Wilderness Battle 23

Chapter 4: "Follow Me" 26

Part II—The Rescue Explained

Chapter 5: Why Micah Believed 33

Chapter 6: Sabbath in Capernaum 36

Chapter 7: Leper No More 39

Chapter 8: Wrecking the Roof 43

Chapter 9: Interrupted by Joy 47

Chapter 10: Peace After the Storm 51

Chapter 11: "Leave Us Alone!" 54

Chapter 12: Two by Two 58

Chapter 13: Walking on the Water 62

Chapter 14: Unexpected Changes 66

Chapter 15: Eyes Covered in Mud 70

Chapter 16: Jesus Is Our Guest 75

Chapter 17: Catching a Coin 79

Chapter 18: A Wealthy Man Wonders 82

Chapter 19: Who Is the Greatest? 87

Chapter 20: The Tree Climber 91

Part III—The Rescue Guaranteed

Chapter 21: The King Rides a Colt 97
Chapter 22: The King Borrows a Room 100
Chapter 23: The King Betrayed 105
Chapter 24: The King Crucified 111
Chapter 25: The King Resurrected 117
Chapter 26: The King's Promise 121

ACKNOWLEDGMENTS

Sincere thanks to the 2021–2022 Redlands Adventist Academy fourth-grade class, their teacher, Denine Matsuda, and to Perla Caraveo. They read the stories, offered suggestions, and helped make *Radical Rescue* a better book! We are grateful. We also appreciate the creative wordsmithing of Jeremy Blaire and Matthew Blaire, who helped craft the title of this book.

We're pleased to have worked with Pacific Press® Publishing Association and continue to be thankful for the dedicated directors, editors, and designers who share their talents and expertise to turn manuscripts into books.

INTRODUCTION

We all love stories of dramatic rescues. Have you ever thought that you can be rescued from the greatest danger of all? Yes, you can be rescued and given a new, wonderful life! And your Rescuer is King of all the universe.

When God created people, He wanted them to be His friends. However, everything changed when Adam and Eve distrusted God and listened to the enemy. They ate the fruit from the tree of knowledge of good and evil. From that moment on God implemented a plan to rescue people from the enemy.

It was a radical plan. It required God's Son to be born as a human being. Isaiah called Him "Immanuel" (Isaiah 7:14) for He would live with people on earth to show them what God is truly like. At the direction of the angel Gabriel, His earthly parents called Him Jesus because He would "save his people from their sins" (Matthew 1:21). The Bible tells us about many, many people Jesus rescued when He left heaven to live on this earth. He ultimately chose to die for us to complete His mission.

This book is a collection of stories about Jesus. Sometimes we added a character or two to help tell the story, and we used our imaginations to think about the people who witnessed the miracles of Jesus, heard His stories, and saw His death, resurrection, and return to heaven. We wanted you to be able to see the stories from their points of view. Always we tried to remain true to the details described in the Bible. Our goal? To write in such a way that everyone who reads this book learns to love Jesus.

We've included questions and activities to encourage you to learn to study the Bible for yourself. Remember to start your Bible study with prayer, asking the Holy Spirit to help you understand better what God would like you to learn. Keep a journal handy. Some of the activities ask you to make journal entries. For others you may want to write down your prayers or your thoughts as you learn more and more about Jesus. There are also discussion starters for conversations with the adults in your life. You'll learn from them and they'll learn from you.

We encourage you to open your Bible to do these things:

Read the original story
We've listed where you can find the story in the Bible so that you can read it. It's important for you to know for yourself exactly what the Bible says.

Compare Bible stories and verses
Here you will find other Bible stories or verses to read that are related to the story in each chapter. One of the ways to study the Bible is to compare what the Bible says in one place with what it says in other places. Think about what these added verses say and how they are similar or different. Try to identify the important lesson.

Answer some questions
We wrote these questions to help focus your thinking. Maybe you have questions you would like to add to the list. Feel free to write them in and talk to a parent, a teacher, a sibling, a pastor, or a friend to sort out information and come up with an answer. It's always an option to ask God for answers too.

Learn a Bible verse
Psalm 119:10, 11 says,

> I seek you with all my heart;
> do not let me stray from your commands.
> I have hidden your word in my heart
> that I might not sin against you.

We encourage you to store these verses in your memory as a way of keeping your heart and mind anchored on Jesus.

Share Jesus with others
Jesus asked us to help share the message of His radical rescue mission. One way to do this is to share what you learn about Jesus from the stories you read. We added activity suggestions to get you started. Can you think of other ways to let people know that God loves them?

As you read about people Jesus radically rescued, remember He wants to do the same for you! It's His greatest gift.

Part I

THE RESCUE WORK BEGINS

Chapter 1

RADICAL RESCUE UNDERSTOOD

Mary had been looking forward to taking Jesus to Passover in Jerusalem for a long time. He hadn't been to the temple since she and Joseph took Him there as a baby to be dedicated. Now, as they were actually on the way, she wondered why He was so quiet. This was the third day of their trip, and soon they would enter Jericho.

"Jesus, do You remember the story about Jericho?" Mary asked.

"Yes, Mother. What a day that was for the Israelites when they finally arrived in the Promised Land," He answered. "Every day for a week, the army of Israel marched around Jericho one time. On the seventh day, they marched around seven times. When all the men shouted together, the walls fell down."

"You're absolutely right. What about Rahab?" Joseph asked.

"Well, Rahab had a house built into the wall of the city. She helped the Israelite spies who had her put a red rope in her window. When Jericho was captured, she and her family were saved. Later, she married someone from the tribe of Judah. She was one of our ancestors," Jesus ended the story.

"Jesus, You have learned Your lessons well. From Jericho, we will climb up the mountains to Jerusalem. We should be there by tomorrow," Joseph said.

"Please tell me about Jerusalem again," Jesus said. "I don't remember anything about it."

"Of course, You don't. You were a very small baby," Mary said.

"Jerusalem has thick walls and massive gates. Herod the Great, who was king when You were born, built himself a very beautiful palace which You will see when we get close to the city," Mary said. "The most magnificent building in Jerusalem is the temple. It was rebuilt when our ancestors came back from Babylon. Herod also has made it bigger and more beautiful. Many say that today it is the loveliest building in all the world. I can't wait for You to see it."

"Didn't King Solomon build the first temple?" Jesus asked.

"Yes, he did. It was destroyed when the Babylonians captured Jerusalem," added Joseph.

Traveling to Jerusalem for the feast was an experience like no other. It took them four or five days to walk from Nazareth. As they traveled along, more and more people joined their group. At night they slept near the road, each family staying together.

Finally, they came to the place where the road went up to Jerusalem. Many steps led up the mountain. Soon, someone in their group started singing,

"I lift up my eyes to the mountains—
  where does my help come from?
My help comes from the LORD,
  the Maker of heaven and earth" (Psalm 121:1, 2).

All the others joined in.

That evening as they sat around the campfire, one of the children asked, "Why do we keep the Passover? What does it mean?"

One of the grandpas told the story of God saving His people from slavery in Egypt. God had told His people through Moses to get ready to leave Egypt. They were to kill a lamb and paint the posts of their doors with its blood. They roasted the lamb and ate it all in one evening. In the morning they all marched out of Egypt on the way to the Promised Land, the country where we live now.

"It was an independence day for us Israelites," said another.

"Soon after, God opened a pathway through the waters of the Red Sea so our fathers and mothers could cross on dry land," someone else commented.

Jesus spoke up, "The lamb had a special meaning too. It reminded everyone in our nation that God's Messiah would come to save His people."

Everyone was quiet. "May that day come soon," many whispered softly.

"We visit the temple to praise God for what He did for our fathers and mothers long ago. We also remember, as Jesus said, that God will send His promised Messiah," said another grandfather.

They all went to sleep, rolled in blankets on the ground, thinking about what God had done for their people.

They awoke to another beautiful spring day. The grass along the road was a vivid green. Flowers bloomed among the rocks and birds sang in the treetops. "Come on, let's go," someone shouted. "We're almost there."

Rounding a corner in the road, they saw Jerusalem ahead of them. It was a beautiful city, crowned with the glorious temple. They stopped walking, moved by the sight of the city. Again, everyone started singing,

"I rejoiced with those who said to me,
  'Let us go to the house of the LORD.'
Our feet are standing
  in your gates, Jerusalem" (Psalm 122:1, 2).

They quickened their steps, anxious to arrive in the city.

Some of their group stayed with family and friends who lived in Jerusalem, but Joseph's family joined many, many others who pitched tents on the slopes around Jerusalem. When the tent was ready, Joseph said, "Come, Jesus. Let me show You the city and the temple. We need to buy a lamb to sacrifice tomorrow for the feast."

Thousands and thousands of people had traveled to Jerusalem for the feast that would begin the next day. The streets were so crowded that people bumped into each other. "Sorry, sorry," they heard people apologizing. Joseph led Jesus to the temple at the hour of the evening sacrifice. They watched as the priest held up a knife to cut the throat of a squirming lamb. The people were quiet and listened to the chants and songs of the Levites, the helpers in the temple; some of them led the music and singing.

Jesus asked Joseph, "The lamb represents Messiah, doesn't he?"

"Yes, Jesus, the lamb represents Messiah," Joseph answered.

The two went to the market to buy a lamb for their Passover dinner. Jesus carried the lamb as they walked through the crowds back to their tent. "Couldn't we just keep the lamb?" Jesus asked as He petted his woolly coat.

"He would make a great pet, wouldn't he," Joseph said, "but a lamb is part of the celebration. He reminds us of what God has done for His people."

Joseph and Mary shared their lamb with some of their relatives because the three of them couldn't eat the whole lamb themselves. The next evening, the family celebrated Passover together with their relatives. The lamb was served with bitter herbs and bread made without yeast, more like crackers than regular bread. The children asked questions about the meaning of Passover. Jesus asked why the lamb had to die, but He didn't seem satisfied with the answers. Together they all recited Psalm 118, which begins and ends with this line, "Give thanks to the Lord, for he is good; his love endures forever" (verses 1, 29).

Later in the evening Mary sat beside Him and whispered softly, "Jesus, You seem so serious. This is a happy occasion."

"Mom, I've been thinking. The lamb dies. In Exodus his blood was painted on the doorposts to save the firstborn son. Doesn't that mean that Messiah must die to save all men?" Jesus whispered back.

"I never thought of it that way, Son," Mary said. "I always thought that Messiah would destroy the Romans who have taken over our country."

"What about the prophecy in Isaiah? Doesn't it say that Messiah must die because of the sins of His people?" Jesus asked (Isaiah 53).

"You have such deep thoughts. You and I must pray for understanding," Mary tried to understand her Son. "Passover is a day of joy to remember how God has blessed our people."

During the week, Joseph and Mary took Jesus to see the important places in Jerusalem. They walked by Herod's palace, visited the pool of Siloam, and climbed the Mount of Olives. Everywhere they asked Jesus questions about the history of His people in that location. Then on the first day of the week the family went to the temple to watch the priest wave the barley sheaf to thank the Lord for the beginning of the harvest. Jesus seemed to enjoy this sign of God's blessing.

Their time in Jerusalem passed quickly. Joseph and Mary with Jesus' help packed up their belongings getting ready for the long walk home. They joined the thousands who left Jerusalem for every part of Judaea and Galilee. The first part of their journey was down the steps to Jericho. They visited with their many friends along the way, rejoicing over the good time they had had at the feast.

When evening came, they found a place for the three of them to sleep. "Where's Jesus?" Mary asked Joseph.

"I thought that He was with you," he answered.

"I thought that He was with you," Mary replied. "He must be here with some of His friends." The two of them hurried, looking at each group of people, asking over and over, "Have you seen Jesus?"

No one had seen Jesus. "Oh, no, we've lost our Son, Jesus. What shall we do?" Mary started to cry.

"Mary, it's getting dark. We can't walk on the road at night. Tomorrow we will start early to go back to look for Him," Joseph tried to comfort Mary. Together they prayed that God would keep their Son safe and that He would show them where to look for Jesus.

In the morning, they hurried up the steps back to Jerusalem. Their friends all called to them, "God will bless you. He will show you where to look. We will pray as we go on to our homes."

The way seemed much longer to Joseph and Mary. They were anxious to find Jesus. Each one prayed, "Please God, help us find Jesus. We never should have let Him out of our sight." By evening they were able to enter Jerusalem before the gates closed. Again, they had to wait for morning to continue their search.

The next day—the third day since they had lost Jesus—they wondered where to look for Him. "Joseph, let's go to the temple. Jesus was fascinated with everything that happened in the temple. He asked so many questions. Maybe He will be there," Mary said.

"Yes, you're right. We'll start at the temple," Joseph agreed with her.

As they came into the temple, they heard a familiar voice, coming from a room with its door ajar. They stopped to listen. Jesus was asking questions.

"If Messiah is to save us from the Romans, why does Isaiah say that He will die for our sins?" He asked (Isaiah 53).

"He asked me that question the night we ate the feast," Mary whispered to Joseph, as they listened to understand who might be answering Him.

They heard the deep voice of a stranger, "My Son, You ask very difficult questions. The lambs we sacrifice represent the Promised One who will save us. Other verses show Messiah to be a mighty warrior. We must all study more to understand how both these things are true. Our people long to be free from the Romans. Passover is to celebrate our independence from Egypt. Why should it not also represent our freedom from the Romans?"

The discussion seemed to be over. Joseph and Mary slipped into the room to see Jesus talking to some well-dressed rabbis. "Jesus, we couldn't find You. We were very worried. We've been looking and looking for You," Mary said.

"Have You been here the whole time? Didn't You realize that the feast was over and it was time to go home?" Joseph added his comments to Mary's.

"Didn't you know that I needed to be about My Father's business?" Jesus answered.

Two of the rabbis came to talk to Mary and Joseph. "Your Son is a remarkable young man. He has never been to our school. We have never seen Him until the day before yesterday. He asks such insightful questions and makes us think deeply," one said.

"Can He stay here and attend our school?" asked the second one.

"We live far from here in Nazareth. I've already missed several days of work because we lost Jesus," Joseph replied, "and I must support my family."

"We would give Him a scholarship and find somewhere He can stay," said the first rabbi.

"Thank you for your kind offer, but He is too young. We need Him with us," Joseph answered. "Come, Jesus, we must get started home."

Jesus left with Joseph and Mary and they started the long walk back to Nazareth. As they walked down the steps again, Mary thought about all that had happened on their trip to Jerusalem. *Does Jesus understand His mission? His questions are so thoughtful that they make me wonder if I truly understand it. Where is God going to lead Him? What will happen to Him and to us?*

When the family got back to Nazareth, Jesus continued to help Joseph in his carpentry shop as He had done before. Neighbors observed what a fine young man Jesus was becoming.

OPEN YOUR BIBLE

Read the original story
Read the story about Jesus' visit to the temple in Luke 2:41–52.

Compare Bible stories and verses
How do Isaiah 53:7 and John 1:29 connect the Passover lamb to Jesus?

Answer some questions
1. How old was Jesus when He went to the Passover?
2. How did going to the Passover in Jerusalem help Jesus understand His radical rescue mission?
3. What do you think Jesus meant when He said, "I needed to be about My Father's business"?

Learn a Bible verse
"But he was pierced for our transgressions, he was crushed for our iniquities; the punishment that brought us peace was on him, and by his wounds we are healed" (Isaiah 53:5).

Share Jesus with others
1. Ask a parent if any of the children in your family were ever lost. Talk about the parent's fear when their child or children were missing. Write in your journal about the lost child.
2. Find a recipe to make unleavened bread. Ask your parent's permission and make the bread. As you eat it, explain to your family what the unleavened bread meant as part of the Passover.
3. Ask an adult you know to tell you how old they were when they understood they were responsible for their own decisions about their friendship with Jesus. Ask them to explain what happened that helped them realize that. How old are you? Have you had a similar experience? Share your story.

Chapter 2

HOPE FOR TOMORROW

Sunlight shone over the hills and danced in the treetops as Lois and Dinah waited for their turn at the village well. Lois used the wait time to tell Dinah all about her recent journey with her husband to hear John the Baptist preach.

"He wears clothes woven from camel hair, with a leather belt around his waist," reported Lois.

"Sounds kind of itchy to me," replied Dinah. "But more important than his clothes, what did he say?"

"Repent! Be baptized! The kingdom of God is at hand!" proclaimed Lois in the style of the famous preacher.

"Who said that?" a third friend, Deborah, interrupted as she poured water from the well into her jar.

"Why, John the Baptist!" explained Dinah. "Lois and her husband were in the crowd at the Jordan River last week."

"Did you get baptized?" asked Deborah.

"My husband and I both did. John's words convinced us we needed to be right with God," said Lois. "John taught that those of us with extra clothes and food should give to people who needed help."

"What else did he say?" asked Dinah.

"Well, there were some tax collectors listening to John speak. They asked John what they should do, and he told them to be honest when they collected money from people."

"That would be a welcome change!" suggested Deborah. "Did any of them get baptized?"

"Oh, yes! Several."

"Well, I hope some of them were the tax collectors from our town," said Dinah. "Seems like every week we have to pay more and more in taxes. It's hardly possible to earn a living these days!"

"Your turn to get water, Lois." Deborah moved out of the way but stayed close to listen.

"Soldiers were baptized too," continued Lois. John instructed them to stop forcing people to give them money and to stop wrongly accusing people of breaking the law."

"Interesting," Deborah commented.

"You should have heard how he answered the Pharisees and Sadducees who asked to be baptized!"

"What?" asked Dinah, eager to hear more of the story.

"He called them a 'brood of vipers' and told them their status as children of Abraham didn't mean anything if their actions didn't match their words."

" 'Brood of vipers?' Pretty strong language," said Dinah.

"Personally, I think the Pharisees and Sadducees were only there to impress the people. You know how they are—lots of show. They asked John if he was the Messiah."

"How did John answer?" asked Deborah.

"He said, 'I am not.' And when they kept asking who he was he said, 'I am the voice of one calling in the wilderness, "Make straight the way for the Lord" ' " (John 1:21, 23).

"I would guess the Pharisees also asked John why he was baptizing. You know how worried they always are about people who threaten their influence," said Deborah.

"Yes! He told them, 'I'm baptizing people in the river. However, there is someone you don't know yet. He is so great I don't deserve the honor of untying his sandals' " (see John 1:26, 27).

"I wonder what John meant. How many days did you stay to hear him speak?" asked Dinah.

"Well, it was quite a journey so we didn't rush back. We camped out one night with some of the others so we could listen to John again the next day. And, that's when things got exciting," claimed Lois.

Dinah started filling her water jar while Lois proceeded with the details.

"The next morning, we went back to hear John preach. We watched him baptize more people. About midafternoon, an ordinary looking Man walked up to John. I heard Him ask to be baptized, but John objected.

" 'I need to be baptized by You!' John replied.

"They had a short conversation, which I didn't hear, and then apparently John agreed to baptize the Man. You'll never guess what happened next!"

"You dropped your shawl into the river and it floated away?" asked Dinah.

"Don't be silly, Dinah. I mean, you'll never guess what happened to the Man."

"Oh," said Dinah.

"Lois, don't make us wait. Just tell us what happened before I have to get back home to make breakfast for my family," insisted Deborah.

The three women started walking back to the village with full water jugs. They waved at their neighbors and smiled at the children playing near the houses.

"Well," continued Lois, "John baptized the Man. When the Man came up out of the water a glowing light seemed to shine all around Him. I saw a dove come down out of the sky and hover above His head. My husband thinks I'm a little crazy, but he was looking at a fisherman who had caught a big fish on the opposite bank of the river and he didn't see anything."

"Was the light bright?" asked Dinah.

"It made me think of the stories our ancestors told about Moses coming down from the mountain of God with the ten commandments, his face glowing."

"Pretty bright, then," commented Deborah.

"There's more! I heard a voice say, 'This is my Son, whom I love; with him I am well pleased' " (Matthew 3:17).

"Was the Man's father in the crowd watching Him get baptized?" asked Dinah.

"No. The voice was from heaven."

"You mean—" gasped Dinah.

"God spoke?" finished Deborah.

"Exactly. Right after I heard the voice, John declared, 'Look, the Lamb of God, who takes away the sin of the world! . . . I have seen and I testify that this is God's Chosen One' " (John 1:29, 34).

They reached Deborah's house first.

"The Messiah? You saw the Messiah?" asked Deborah.

"Hallelujah! Soon we'll be free from the Romans!" exclaimed Dinah.

"I truly believe I saw the Messiah. But, I'm not sure about the Roman government part. I keep thinking about John's statement: 'Look, the Lamb of God, who takes away the sin of the world!' [John 1:29]. It doesn't sound like the Messiah's mission has anything to do with freeing us from the Romans."

"I want to hear more," said Deborah, "but I have work to do now."

"Me too!" added Dinah. "Just knowing the Messiah is here makes me happy. I wonder if He will visit our village one day."

"We'll keep our ears to the news—if He's anywhere near we'll go out to meet Him," suggested Lois. "Maybe He would bless our children if we asked. See you tomorrow, my friends! Bye!"

"Bye, Lois. Thanks for sharing your story!" called Deborah. "See you in the morning."

All three women returned to their homes, their hearts full of hope and their heads full of dreams for a future made better by the Messiah.

OPEN YOUR BIBLE

Read the original story

Find the story of John preaching to the people and baptizing Jesus in Matthew 3:1–17; Mark 1:1–11; Luke 3:1–22; and John 1:19–34.

Compare Bible stories and verses

After you read the four accounts of Jesus' baptism in Matthew, Mark, Luke, and John, think about them. How are they similar? Are there differences?

Answer some questions

1. Why was Lois so excited to tell her friends about what she and her husband witnessed at the Jordan River?
2. Why do you think the dove is important to this story?
3. How does John's description of Jesus, "the Lamb of God," share the idea of Jesus' mission to radically rescue people on earth?

Learn a Bible verse

"The next day John saw Jesus coming toward him and said, 'Look, the Lamb of God, who takes away the sin of the world!' " (John 1:29).

Share Jesus with others

1. Use a Bible dictionary to research what the symbol of a dove means to a Christian. Use a Bible concordance to find five verses in the Bible that have the word *dove* in them. What is the importance of the word *dove* in each verse? Add this information to your journal.
2. Paint or draw a picture of a dove hovering over Jesus' head at His baptism. Use what you learned in the previous activity to write a caption for the picture. Share your picture.
3. John called Jesus the "Lamb of God." Read the story of the Passover lamb in Exodus 12. Make a list in your journal of how you see that Jesus is like the Passover lamb. In what ways does this list help you better understand Jesus' mission to radically rescue you?

Chapter 3

THE WILDERNESS BATTLE

Angels watched as Jesus was baptized and then led by the Holy Spirit into the hot, barren desert.* However, they knew He was safe because He was talking with His Father. The Father's presence gave Jesus strength to go without food for forty days because God is the Source of all life. Their conversations gave Jesus encouragement and direction as He was about to begin His radical mission to rescue people on earth from the enemy, Satan.

However, the angels were on guard when the conversations ended and they saw Satan make a move toward Jesus.

Satan was named Lucifer when he lived in heaven, but that was before he started the war. At first, Lucifer had been the highest angel, but then he started thinking that he should be equal with God. So, he began spreading rumors saying that God wasn't fair, His laws were unjust and impossible to follow, and God couldn't be trusted. It was a terrible and confusing time.

Eventually, the day came when everyone had to choose whom to trust—Lucifer or God. Sadly, one-third of the angels chose to trust Lucifer, and they were all removed from heaven (see Revelation 12). After Lucifer—now called Satan—convinced Adam and Eve that God couldn't be trusted, he claimed earth as his rightful kingdom.

As the angels watched Satan approach Jesus in the desert, they wondered what his plan was. They knew better than to trust him. They knew Satan wanted to destroy Jesus—or at least ruin the mission. After all, Satan had tried to use Herod's soldiers to kill Jesus when He was a tiny baby. But an angel warned Joseph and they escaped to Egypt (Matthew 2:13–15). And now, they were again ready to help Jesus the moment the Father sent them. For now, the command was to wait and watch.

Satan, appearing like an angel of light, walked up to Jesus and said, "If you are the Son of God, tell these stones to become bread" (Matthew 4:3).

Talk about unfair! Jesus hadn't eaten for forty days! But, unsurprisingly, this was the same trick Satan had used in heaven and in the Garden of Eden—making the

* See Matthew 4:11 and Ellen G. White, *The Desire of Ages* (Nampa, ID: Pacific Press®, 2005), 131.

angels and Adam and Eve wonder, *Can God be trusted?* Forty days ago, God told Jesus at His baptism, "You are my Son" (Luke 3:22). Would Jesus doubt Him now?

Jesus looked at Satan and said, "It is written: 'Man shall not live on bread alone, but on every word that comes from the mouth of God' " (Matthew 4:4).

The smile on Satan's face faded, and his eyes narrowed.

The watching angels stayed focused on the scene. Each one wondered, *What will Satan do next?*

Next, Satan took Jesus to the top of the temple in Jerusalem.

> "If you are the Son of God, . . . throw yourself down. For it is written:
>
> " 'He will command his angels concerning you,
> and they will lift you up in their hands,
> so that you will not strike your foot against a stone' " (Matthew 4:6).

Once more Satan tried to plant that seed of doubt, "*If* you are the Son of God . . ."

But Jesus didn't have to prove anything to Satan or anyone else. He responded, "It is also written: 'Do not put the Lord your God to the test' " (Matthew 4:7). Jesus knew He was the Son of God, and He knew that God can be trusted.

Then Satan took Jesus to a high mountain where he showed Jesus all of the kingdoms on earth. There the devil highlighted all of the glorious achievements of humankind. And then Satan revealed the pride and evil that filled his heart, "All this I will give you, . . . if you will bow down and worship me" (Matthew 4:9).

There it was—the "I want to be equal with God" desire that turned Lucifer into Satan. God created everything. How could a created being think that he could be equal with God? And what unrepentant pride to ask his Creator to bow down to him!

The heavenly witnesses watched closely, knowing that if Jesus bowed to Satan, the radical rescue mission would be lost—forever.

Jesus' voice echoed across the hilltops, "Away from me, Satan! For it is written: 'Worship the Lord your God, and serve him only' " (Matthew 4:10).

The watching angels rejoiced—their glorious Commander had won! They knew that the devil would continue to try to defeat Jesus' mission, but a major battle was won that day. For Satan has to leave at Jesus' command. He raged angrily as he left, but he had no power to stay and tempt Jesus any longer.

At last, the Father sent His angels, "Go and help Jesus!" And they flew to His side! They cared for Jesus, and assured Him that all of heaven loved Him and rejoiced in His victory.*

---

* See Matthew 4:11 and Ellen G. White, *The Desire of Ages* (Nampa, ID: Pacific Press®, 2005), 131.

The food and companionship strengthened Him. It wasn't long before He continued on to complete His first task of choosing disciples.

The angels didn't completely understand why the Creator left heaven to walk among men. However, they knew without a doubt that the radical rescue mission proved that God can be trusted.

OPEN YOUR BIBLE

Read the original story
Find the story about the battle between Jesus and Satan in Matthew 4:1–11.

Compare Bible stories and verses
Luke also wrote the story of Jesus being tempted in Luke 4:1–13. Why do you think parts of Luke and Matthew's stories are the same and others are different?

Answer some questions
1. What three things did Satan ask Jesus to do?
2. What tool did Jesus use to answer Satan that you can also use to resist temptation?
3. Why was this confrontation so important to Jesus' radical mission of rescuing people?

Learn a Bible verse
"For we do not have a high priest who is unable to empathize with our weaknesses, but we have one who has been tempted in every way, just as we are—yet he did not sin. Let us then approach God's throne of grace with confidence, so that we may receive mercy and find grace to help us in our time of need" (Hebrews 4:15, 16).

Share Jesus with others
1. In your journal, make a chart with three columns. In the first column, list the temptations Jesus experienced in this story. In the second column, write some temptations you face that are similar to Jesus' temptations. In the third column, write the words Jesus quoted from the Bible to answer Satan. Ask God to help you remember Jesus' answers when you are tempted.
2. Write a story about a time you were tempted and how you were able to resist the temptation. Share your story with a friend.
3. Do you know someone who is struggling to make good choices? Write a prayer in your journal asking God to give that person strength and wisdom to resist the temptation.

Chapter 4

"FOLLOW ME"

"Are you the Christ, the one God promised would come?" one of the Pharisees asked the man dressed in a robe made of camel's hair.

John and Andrew waited hopefully for his answer. They, along with Andrew's brother, Simon Peter, had walked all the way from Galilee to listen to John the Baptist preach. They wanted to know if John the Baptist was the Christ too.

"No, someone so great that I'm not worthy to unfasten His sandals is here in the crowd today," John answered.

"Well, if you are not the Christ, why are you here at the Jordan River baptizing people?" the questioner asked.

"I am a voice, crying in the wilderness, prepare the way of the Lord," John said (see Isaiah 40:3).

Andrew and John looked carefully at the crowd of listeners, wondering which one was the great Person John had mentioned. That evening they talked with Andrew's brother, Simon Peter.

"Simon, John the Baptist said that there was someone in the crowd who is so great he isn't worthy to unfasten the Man's sandal. We looked carefully but the only ones who looked important were those Pharisees in their fancy robes who were questioning John," said Andrew.

"Maybe the Baptizer will give us some more clues tomorrow," said Simon.

"We must go early tomorrow morning to hear him again," said John.

The next day they listened to John the Baptist preach again. This time he pointed to a man in the crowd, saying, "Look, the Lamb of God, who takes away the sin of the world [John 1:29]. I saw the Holy Spirit as a dove rest on Him. I know that He is the Son of God."

The third day, Andrew and John listened to the Baptizer's preaching. "Look, the Lamb of God," he said, pointing to a man (John 1:36).

"Come," Andrew said to John, "we must follow Him." This time, they were sure which Man John the Baptist meant. They slipped through the crowd until they were right behind the Man John had pointed out.

The Man turned to them and said, "What do you want?"

"Where are You staying?" they asked.

"Come and see," He responded.

Andrew and John followed Him. "I am Jesus of Nazareth," He told them. They spent the afternoon talking to Him. Sometimes others stopped to listen. Andrew wanted to listen to Jesus forever, but he slipped away to find Simon.

"Simon, Simon, we have found the Messiah. Come with me. You must hear Him too," Andrew urged his brother.

When the two arrived back at the place where Jesus was talking, Jesus said to Simon, "You are Simon, but you will be called Peter."

* * * * *

The next morning, Jesus told them, "Some of My relatives are getting married in Cana. I must go to the wedding."

"May we come too?" Peter asked.

"Yes, I want you to follow Me," Jesus answered.

Before they left for Cana, Jesus stopped a man named Philip and said, "Follow Me."

Philip was so happy that he hurried off to find his friend Nathanael. He knew that Nathanael had also been listening to John the Baptist and was praying that God would show him if he should follow the Man that the Baptizer had pointed out. Finding his friend sitting under a fig tree and praying, Philip called, "Nathanael, I've found the Messiah, the one Moses wrote about. He's Jesus of Nazareth."

"Nazareth! Can anything good come from there?" Nathanael asked (John 1:46).

"Come and see," Philip answered.

Nathanael went with Philip to find Jesus. When Jesus saw Nathanael coming, He said, "Here is a man of Israel who always tells the truth."

"How do You know me?" Nathanael asked.

"I saw you when you were sitting under the fig tree," Jesus answered.

"Rabbi, I believe! You are the Son of God!" Nathanael said.

"Oh, Nathanael. You believe because I said that I saw you under the fig tree. You will see greater things than this," Jesus said.

Jesus called the others, "Follow Me." Together they left for Cana and the wedding.

* * * * *

Sometime later, Jesus was in Capernaum. In the early morning He walked by the lake, hoping to spend some time praying and relaxing. He noticed Peter and Andrew cleaning their nets after a night of fishing. "Good catch?" He asked.

"Nothing," Peter answered. "We fished all night and caught nothing."

"Kind of discouraging," Andrew added.

John and his brother, James, were also nearby cleaning their nets.

Jesus walked on, noticing the morning sunshine sparkling on the lake. Soon other people saw Jesus and followed Him. Jesus came back and called out, "Hey Peter, Andrew, can I borrow your boat?

"Sure," they answered.

Jesus climbed in the boat and rowed out a little way. He sat down in the boat and preached to the growing crowd. The audience listened intently.

When the sermon was over, Jesus went over to talk to Peter and Andrew. "Take the boat and throw out your net," He told them.

"We fished all night and caught nothing. The water in this lake is so clear that fishing has to be done at night, when the fish can't see the net. But, because You said it, we will follow Your directions," they said.

When the brothers cast out their net, they caught so many fish that their boat was about to sink. "Help! Help!" they called. "James! John! Our boat is about to sink!"

John and James rowed their boat over quickly and transferred many of the fish to it. Neither boat sank. As they reached the shore, Peter jumped out of his and Andrew's boat, ran to Jesus and bowed at His feet. "Jesus, Jesus, I'm a sinful man. Go away from me," he said, all the time clinging to Jesus' feet.

"Follow Me, and I'll make you fishers of men. You will lead many to believe in Me," Jesus told Peter and the others (Matthew 4:19).

From that day forward, all four of them left their boats and nets to follow Jesus wherever He went.

* * * * *

Another day as Jesus was walking by the lake, He passed a tax collector's booth. The tax collector's name was Levi Matthew. He had heard about Jesus and would have liked to meet Him, but he thought that Jesus would be like the Pharisees who hated tax collectors and refused to talk to him.

Instead, Jesus smiled at Matthew and said, "Follow Me."

Matthew was amazed; but he left his tax booth and followed Jesus. Because Matthew was so pleased to be invited to be one of Jesus' disciples, he decided to have a big feast in honor of Jesus. Matthew was rich and had a big house. He invited all his friends to come to the feast to meet Jesus. Since the "good" people of the town would never come to Matthew's house, he invited those who were considered to be the "bad" people. He invited other tax collectors and thieves, crooks, and Roman pleasers.

When the Pharisees saw Matthew's guests, they decided to make trouble for Jesus. "This is our chance. We will criticize Jesus to His disciples. Then they won't want to follow Him anymore," they said to each other.

As Jesus and His disciples walked to Matthew's house for the feast along with the other guests, some of the Pharisees pulled Peter and John over to talk to them. "Why is Jesus going to eat with these tax collectors and sinners?" they asked. The Pharisees believed that no decent person would be around people like Matthew and his guests.

Jesus heard their question and answered, "It's sick people who go to doctors, not those who are well. I haven't come to call 'good' people, but 'sinners' to repentance" (see Matthew 9:12).

The Pharisees didn't know how to respond to Jesus. They shut their mouths and went away, trying to think of a way to trick Him at their next opportunity.

Everywhere Jesus went, His disciples followed Him.

OPEN YOUR BIBLE

Read the original story

Read the following Bible passages to learn more about how Jesus called His disciples in Matthew 3; 4:18–22; Mark 1:4–20; Luke 3:1–22; 5:1–11, 27, 28; and John 1:15–51.

Compare Bible stories and verses

Read about when God called Moses to lead His people out of Egypt in Exodus 3. How is the story like Jesus' calling His disciples and how is it different?

Answer some questions

1. Why did John and Andrew want to learn more about Jesus?
2. How did Nathanael realize that Jesus was the Messiah?
3. How did Matthew's friends learn about God's radical rescue plan?

Learn a Bible verse

" 'Come, follow me,' Jesus said, 'and I will send you out to fish for people' " (Matthew 4:19).

Share Jesus with others

1. Draw a series of pictures to illustrate this story. Use word bubbles to show what the different characters say. Put them together to make a booklet and share your booklet with family or friends.
2. Talk to an adult about what it means to follow Jesus and about how to become a fisher of people.
3. If you have been baptized, write a journal entry, explaining what your baptism meant to you. If you have not been baptized, imagine what the day will mean to you, and write about it—and think about asking to be baptized soon!

Part II

THE RESCUE EXPLAINED

Chapter 5

WHY MICAH BELIEVED

Micah, the king's official, hurried up the last hill to Cana. It had been a long trip, twenty miles almost all uphill from Capernaum. *The only way I'll believe that Jesus is the Messiah is if He heals Joel,* he thought.

As he entered the town, Micah noticed a large group of people. He wondered why they were all together and hoped that in this crowd he'd find the Man he was searching for. He listened to the people around him, talking excitedly, "Did you see what He did in the temple?"

"No, I couldn't go to the feast."

"He made the people selling animals and changing money leave the temple because He spoke with such authority. They grabbed their animals and their money boxes and ran out of the temple."

"That would have been something to see!"

Micah turned to one of the men standing beside him. "I heard that Jesus came here to Cana. Do you know where I can find Him?"

"He's right here," the man pointed to someone in a blue robe, talking to a group of people. "Would you like for me to introduce you to Him?"

"You know Him?" Micah answered. "He looks so ordinary. I thought that Jesus would be the tallest man around, wearing fancy clothes. How do you know Him anyway?"

"I'm Andrew, one of Jesus' disciples," the man answered. "Jesus is a really wonderful Man, but He is unusual in what He says and what He does, not in how He looks."

"My little boy is very, very sick. The doctor says that he probably will die. I need to talk to Jesus," Micah said.

"Don't worry. Jesus specializes in healing people. I think He especially likes to heal children," Andrew said. "Come with me. I'll take you to see Jesus."

Micah and Andrew walked through the crowd. Jesus noticed them coming and smiled a welcome. "Jesus, I want You to meet—" he paused and turned to Micah.

"My name is Micah."

"Micah has an important request," Andrew told Jesus.

"Jesus, please come with me to Capernaum. My young son is very ill. The doctor says that he will die," Micah pleaded.

"Unless you see miracles, you will not believe," Jesus answered. Suddenly Micah knew that Jesus spoke the truth.

"I'm sorry, Master. I had told myself that I only would believe if Joel is healed," Micah admitted.

"Your son is healed. You can go home in peace," Jesus said.

"Yes, Jesus, I know that You have healed Joel. I do believe. You are the Promised One, the Messiah, our Savior," Micah felt so relieved.

Jesus started talking to the people. Micah stayed to listen. Later, he started the long walk home to Capernaum; but he didn't mind the length, to him it was a glorious day. In everything—the sky, the sunshine, the singing birds, and the brilliant flowers—he saw God's love. He was excited about getting home to see what Jesus had done.

Micah didn't arrive home until the next day. His servants were watching for him, and when they saw him coming, they ran to meet him. "Master, master," they cried. "Wonderful news! Joel is well."

"I know," Micah called to them. "Jesus healed him. When did he start to get better?"

"It was yesterday at the seventh hour. All of a sudden, the fever left him and he got up to play," the servants explained.

"That was just the time Jesus said that Joel was healed," Micah told them. "Isn't Jesus wonderful?"

"Where is my wife? Where is Joel? I must see them," Micah continued.

As Micah and the servants neared the house, Joel came running to meet them. "Daddy, I'm well," Joel shouted, running to hug his father.

Micah's wife hurried out of the house, "Micah, look, Joel is well!" she exclaimed.

Micah hugged her too. "I have a story to tell you. Yesterday I talked to Jesus. He said that Joel would live. Truly Jesus is the Messiah. We must follow Him."

Micah and his family told many people in Capernaum about how Jesus had healed Joel and that they were sure that Jesus was the Promised One. When Jesus and His disciples came to preach in that town, many people already believed in Jesus because of Joel's witness.

OPEN YOUR BIBLE

Read the original story

Read the story about the ruler's son being healed in John 4:46–54.

Compare Bible stories and verses

Read about Jesus healing the centurion's servant in Matthew 8:5–13 and Luke 7:1–10. In Mark 7:31–37 is a story about Jesus healing a man who was both deaf and mute. What similarities or differences do you notice?

Answer some questions

1. Why did Micah make the long walk to Cana?
2. Before Micah met Jesus, what did he decide would be the only reason he would believe that Jesus was the Messiah?
3. What convinces you to believe in the power of Jesus to radically rescue you?

Learn a Bible verse

"Lord my God, I called to you for help, and you healed me" (Psalm 30:2).

Share Jesus with others

1. Talk to an adult about why Jesus told Micah that he would only believe if he saw Jesus work a miracle for Joel. Why does Jesus want us to have faith in Him even if we don't see a miracle?
2. Make a collection of video interviews with people you know. Ask them to share about a time they asked God to answer their prayers. Some will have received a yes in answer to their prayers. Some will have received a no in answer to their prayers. Ask them to explain how they felt and whether the answer to their prayers changed their belief in God. Why or why not?
3. Imagine that you are Joel. Write in your journal about your sickness and how you suddenly got well before your father returned. Add to your story what Joel thinks once he hears the story of his father's conversation with Jesus.

Chapter 6

SABBATH IN CAPERNAUM

Andrew walked with Jesus and the other disciples to the synagogue in Capernaum one Sabbath morning. He noticed a boy and a man waving at him. When he looked closer, he recognized Micah.

"Hello, Andrew," Micah said, as he came over to talk to Andrew. "I want you to meet my son, Joel. He's the one Jesus healed. Joel, I want you to meet Andrew. He's the one who introduced me to Jesus the day you were healed."

"Hello, Joel," Andrew said, shaking the child's hand.

"Andrew, will you introduce me to Jesus too?" Joel asked.

Andrew took Joel's hand and led him to Jesus. "Jesus, this is Joel. He's the boy you healed a couple of weeks ago. Here's his father, Micah."

Jesus stooped down so His face was level with Joel's. "I'm glad that you're well. Will you become My follower?"

"I'm already Your follower. I tell everyone I meet that You healed me," Joel answered.

Jesus gave the boy a hug and they all walked into the synagogue.

Joel and his father sat on one of the benches to listen to Jesus' preaching. Joel whispered to Micah, "I can understand everything that Jesus says. I will be His follower forever."

The worshipers listened intently to Jesus. He taught differently than the rabbis. The way He explained the scriptures made so much sense. The people in the synagogue would have liked for Him to speak much longer.

Suddenly, a man who had been sitting in the back, came hurrying to the front, shouting loudly, "Go away! What do you want with us, Jesus of Nazareth? Have you come to destroy us? I know who you are—the Holy One of God!" (Luke 4:34).

"Be quiet!" Jesus said in a stern voice. "Come out of him!" (Luke 4:35). The man shook as the impure spirit left him. "Trust in God and follow His Word," Jesus told the man.

The people in the synagogue were shocked and excited. "Jesus is amazing," they cried.

"Look at all the people He has healed."

"When He teaches, God's Word makes sense."

"Jesus has cast the impure spirit from this man."

"It's unbelievable what Jesus has done."

"Do you think that He is the Messiah, God's Promised One?"

Jesus and the disciples left the synagogue quietly to go to Peter's house which was nearby. As they were leaving, Andrew noticed Joel and his father, Micah. Jesus saw them, too, and waved to Joel.

As they entered Peter's house, his wife motioned to them to be quiet. "Sh! Sh!" she said.

"My mother is sick with a high fever."

"Where is she?" Jesus asked.

Peter's wife led Jesus to her mother's bed. When Jesus touched her hand, she sat up in bed, looked around, and thanked Jesus. "I need to get out of bed so I can help you fix lunch for all these men," she told her daughter.

That afternoon, after the lunch provided by Peter's family, Jesus and the disciples rested quietly.

In the evening after sunset when the Sabbath was over, many people came to the house looking for Jesus. "We heard what You did for that little boy, Joel. We saw what happened at the synagogue this morning. Please heal us now too."

Many came with every sort of disease. Some had fevers; some walked with a cane; some were blind; some were deaf. Some were children; some were mothers and fathers; and some were very old. Everyone wanted to be blessed and healed by Jesus, and He talked to each one and gave the needed healing.

As they waited, people talked excitedly about Jesus. Some thought that Jesus was the Messiah. Some thought that He would make the Romans leave their country. Some thought that theirs could be the only country with no sick people. At last, when Jesus had cared for each person, they all went home.

Very tired, Jesus lay down to sleep, but early in the morning while it was still dark, He left the house to go to a place where He could pray alone. After the sun came up and the people in Capernaum got up for the day, Andrew, Peter, and some of the disciples went searching for Jesus.

"Everyone is looking for You," the men told Jesus, when they found Him.

"We need to go to the nearby villages. Many others need to be healed and to hear our message," Jesus told them.

Jesus walked on ahead as they went back to the house. Peter said to the others, "I was hoping Jesus would stay longer here in Capernaum because the people want to listen to Him."

"Maybe His mission is different from what we expect," Andrew said. "He would make a wonderful King, but I think He has something different in mind."

"We will have to wait and watch so we can follow where He leads us, instead of expecting Him to do what we want," said another disciple.

Later as they started walking down the road to another town, Joel was standing by the road. "Jesus, are You going away? I will miss You," the boy called.

"Joel, there are other boys and girls who need Me to talk to them and make them well too," Jesus said.

"God go with You, Jesus," Joel answered.

"And God bless you, Joel," Jesus waved goodbye.

OPEN YOUR BIBLE

Read the original story

Read the story about the Sabbath in Capernaum in Luke 4:31–44 and Mark 1:21–39.

Compare Bible stories and verses

Read about other people that Jesus healed on Sabbath in Mark 3:1–6 and John 5:1–18.

Answer some questions

1. Why did many people wait until the Sabbath was over before coming to Peter's house to be healed?
2. Why did Jesus say He couldn't stay in Capernaum?
3. How could Jesus make the impure spirit leave the man who was possessed?

Learn a Bible verse

"Heal me, LORD, and I will be healed; save me and I will be saved, for you are the one I praise" (Jeremiah 17:14).

Share Jesus with others

1. Research to discover what you can learn about synagogues in the time of Jesus. Write about your findings in your journal and discuss them with an adult.
2. Talk to a health-care worker and ask them to describe how they feel they are following Jesus' example of healing when they work with their patients.
3. In Luke 14:5, Jesus asks the people who witness His Sabbath healing, "If one of you has a child or an ox that falls into a well on the Sabbath day, will you not immediately pull it out?" Talk with your family about how this principle applies to your lives.

Chapter 7

Leper No More

Jeremy sat in the shade, watching someone walking along the path that led to his cave. *That tall young man could be Reuben, my son. He's bringing a basket. Maybe it's for me.* About 100 feet from the cave the slim figure laid a basket on a stone and then turned to look straight at Jeremy. He waved. Jeremy waved back. It was Reuben! Reuben started back the way he had come. Jeremy ran to get the basket.

For a leper, I am very lucky. Most of my fellow lepers' families have forgotten about them. My wife sends me food, sometimes warm clothes, and a message several times a week. I must thank God for such a good family, he thought. In the basket there was food, always lots of food, enough to share with his fellow lepers. A piece of pottery had a note written on it.

Jeremy reached for the pottery first. The note said: "Anna, our daughter, is getting married in two months to Samuel Bar Jonah. Love, Rosalie." *Anna was only five when I had to leave home because of this terrible leprosy. Has it really been so long? I will miss my own daughter's wedding.*

Jeremy forced himself to be cheerful for his friends' sake. "Hey, fellows, my wife sent us some food. Come and eat."

The other lepers came to the front of the cave and waited patiently while Jeremy gave each of them some of the food. One reminded the others to thank God for the food. While they ate, one of the men told the others, "I have heard that Jesus has come to our town. He heals people with all kinds of diseases."

"Do you think that He could heal leprosy?" another man asked.

"I don't know."

"Maybe He could," a hopeful voice chimed in.

"I want to see Him."

That night as the others were sleeping, Jeremy prayed silently, "Please, Lord, help me find Jesus."

Early in the morning, Jeremy slipped away by himself. He knew that people who saw him would be afraid. He was required to wear clothes that were torn and could not comb his hair. He had been a leper for so long that parts of his fingers were missing and part of his nose as well. He knew that he looked awful, but he was determined to ignore the stares. And he would call out "Unclean," when anyone came near. Yes, some would be afraid of him, but he *had* to see Jesus.

People were gathered on a hillside, watching someone at the bottom of the hill. Jeremy stayed behind everyone else and no one came near him. He listened to the conversations around him as much as he could hear from a distance.

"That's Jesus," a man said.

"Maybe He'll heal someone," his companion added.

Jeremy saw a man, carrying a child, walk up to Jesus. Jesus said something that Jeremy could not hear, then he touched the child, and the child sat up, jumped down from his father's arms, and started running in circles. A woman, leaning on a cane, slowly approached Jesus who spoke to her. Jeremy watched her drop the cane and start dancing.

A woman came forward, leading a man who appeared to be blind. The man spoke to Jesus, who touched his eyes. The man shouted, "I can see! I can see! Thank You, Jesus!"

Jeremy became more and more excited. He turned to someone who backed away from him, asking, "Can Jesus heal a leper?"

At the word leper people turned, looked at Jeremy and moved away from him. Noticing the people's desire to avoid him, he thought, *I don't care. I* will *talk to Jesus.*

He started pushing his way, faster and faster, down to the hill to Jesus. People shoved each other to get away from this ugly, dirty leper. Jeremy rushed up to Jesus and fell on his knees before Him. "Jesus, if You want to, You can heal me, a leper."

"I am willing," Jesus answered. "Be clean!" (Luke 5:13).

At once Jeremy's appearance changed. His fingers were whole and straight. His nose looked like it did when he was well. The crowd who had pushed themselves away from Jeremy stood with their mouths open in amazement.

"God be praised!" Jeremy yelled.

Jesus spoke to him softly. "You must go show yourself to the priest so he will see that you no longer have leprosy. Take the offering that is mentioned in the Torah. Don't tell anyone what happened here today."

Jeremy turned around, ready to go to the priest. A voice in the crowd called loudly, "Is that you, Jeremy?" It was Rosalie, his wife. She had come to see and hear Jesus, along with Reuben and Anna.

He heard two voices, one low and one high, yelling "*Abba! Abba!*"*

* Daddy! Daddy!

Rosalie and her excited children pushed through the crowd to hug her husband and their father.

"Go to the priest. Take Reuben with you. Anna and I will go home to find you some clean clothes and make your favorite dinner. Praise God. Today we have seen a real miracle."

As Reuben and Jeremy started to go to see the priest, Anna called, "Abba, now you can come to my wedding!"

OPEN YOUR BIBLE

Read the original story
Read the story about Jesus healing the leper in Matthew 8:1–4; Mark 1:40–45; and Luke 5:12–16.

Compare Bible stories and verses
Read Luke 17:11–19 to find the story of Jesus healing ten lepers. How is that story the same and how is it different?

Answer some questions
1. Why couldn't Jeremy live with his family?
2. Why did Jeremy have to go to see the priest?
3. How was the healing of Jeremy like the radical rescue mission of Jesus to forgive people?

Learn a Bible verse
"If we confess our sins, he is faithful and just and will forgive us our sins and purify us from all unrighteousness" (1 John 1:9).

Share Jesus with others
1. Research to find information about leprosy. Draw a picture of the man with leprosy. Then draw a second picture of the man after he was healed. Share your pictures and tell Jeremy's story.
2. Talk to some of your friends or siblings about the story of the leper's healing. Together imagine what the story must have seemed like to people who were watching. Then act out the story of Jesus healing the leper for an audience. Ask the people in the audience to tell you what the story means to them.
3. Find a white board, marker, and eraser or cloth. Fill the white board with drawings or words. Use the white board to create a worship talk about forgiveness. Show how the white board can be completely cleaned with the

eraser or cloth. Remind your listeners that because of His radical rescue mission, Jesus can forgive completely just like the white board can be cleaned completely. Use a Bible concordance to find a Bible verse about forgiveness to complete your lesson. Share your worship talk.

Chapter 8

WRECKING THE ROOF

"Have you heard?" Tabor asked his friend Justus as he entered the little house, "I just saw Jesus in the market. He was walking down toward the lake."

"I would like to see Jesus. Have you heard about all the wonderful things He does?" Justus answered as he lay on a mat on the floor.

"Yes, just the other day He healed a leper—a *leper!* That would have been something to see," Tabor said.

"Do you think that He would heal me?" Justus asked.

"Why wouldn't He heal you?" Tabor asked in reply.

"Because the rabbi wouldn't pray for me. He said that my illness was the result of all the bad things I did," Justus said. "And I think that he's right. I did do a lot of bad things. I'd be happy if I knew that God forgives me," Justus sighed and wiped a tear from his eye.

"Did you ask God to forgive you?" Tabor said.

"Yes, but I don't have the money to buy a sacrifice in Jerusalem," Justus explained.

"We could ask Jesus to heal you. He might say yes. He would know whether God will forgive you," his friend continued.

"Look at me, Tabor. I'm paralyzed. I can't walk. How will I find Jesus?" Justus laid his head back on his pillow.

"OK, Justus. This is what I will do. I will find our friends, Achim, Daire, and Galim to help me carry you on your mat. Besides, I need to find out where Jesus was going," Tabor closed the door of the little house, calling back to Justus. "I'll be right back."

Tabor found his friends at the market. "Have you seen Jesus?" he asked them.

"I saw Him go into Peter's house by the lake of Galilee," Achim answered.

"Lots of people were following Him, even some of the rabbis and Pharisees," added Daire. "The house must be crammed full of people."

"Have you been to see Justus recently?" Tabor asked.

"It's been several weeks," said Galim.

"Same, here," Daire added.

"It's been quite a while," said Achim.

"I just came from his house. He looks much worse, and I'm afraid that he will die soon," Tabor told them.

"Oh, no," they all said. "What can we do to help?"

"He can't walk anymore. The rabbi refused to pray for him because his sickness is caused by his sins. Justus asked God to forgive him, but he doesn't have the money for a sacrifice at the temple," Tabor explained. "Please help me carry him to Jesus. It's his only hope."

"Of course, of course, we'll help," they all said. Achim turned to close up his shop and Daire did the same.

"I have some ropes that we can tie to the corners of his mat," Galim added. "I'll run home and get them and meet you at Justus's house."

The three men walked the short distance to their friend's house. As they went into the house, Tabor noticed the sad but surprised looks on his friends' faces as they saw Justus on his mat.

"Justus, we've come to take you to see Jesus," Achim said.

"Galim's coming with some ropes that we can tie to the corners of your mat, to make it easier to carry you," said Daire.

"Thank you, my friends," Justus said. "Could one of you bring the water jug and help me wash my face? I need a clean face to see Jesus."

Galim brought the ropes. Each man made holes in the mat so a rope could be securely tied to the corners of Justus's mat. They picked him up, mat and all, and went out the door. "Are you comfortable, Justus?" asked Galim.

"I'm OK," Justus answered. "But I don't care. Seeing Jesus is all that matters."

When they came to Peter's house, many people crowded around outside, trying to catch a glimpse of Jesus or hear some of His words. Tabor thought there was no way that they could carry their friend into the house. It seemed there was no chance to see Jesus.

"I have an idea," said Justus. "Can you carry me up the stairs onto the roof? You could break the roof and let me down inside the house." Houses in Israel had flat roofs that could be used for extra rooms. Sometimes people slept on their roofs on hot summer nights.

"What a unique idea!" said Achim.

"I guess we could," said Galim.

"Why not?" said Daire.

"Great idea!" said Tabor. "Let's do it."

They pushed through the crowd, carrying Justus on the mat, and climbed the stairs. The men set Justus down on the roof. Someone from below said, "Here, you can use my hammer."

Another in the crowd hollered, "What are you doing?"

"Can't you see?" asked another. "They want Jesus to heal the sick man. The roof is their only way to get into the house."

Tabor and his friends opened a hole in the roof. Jesus' kind face looked up at them. They enlarged the hole to make it big enough to let Justus down. "Hey, Peter, we'll fix the roof," called Tabor.

The four men carefully lowered their friend into the room below. Jesus, smiling at Justus, touched his hand. "Son, your sins are forgiven," He said (Mark 2:5).

Tabor whispered to his friends, "Look at Justus's face. Forgiveness is what he wanted the most." Then the four friends noticed the scowling faces of the rabbis and Pharisees in contrast to Justus's contented smile.

"Which is easier: to say to this paralyzed man, 'Your sins are forgiven,' or to say, 'Get up, take your mat and walk'? But I want you to know that the Son of Man has authority on earth to forgive sins," Jesus said to the men scowling at Him (Mark 2:9, 10).

Jesus turned, to Justus again and said, "I tell you, get up, take your mat and go home" (Mark 2:11).

Justus stood up, rolled up his mat, and tied the ropes around it as his friends walked down the outdoor stairway. "Thank You, Jesus," he said aloud. Justus walked out the front door as everyone, inside and outside the house, shouted, "Praise God. Hallelujah! We have never seen anything like this."

Justus jumped up and down, spread out his arms, and shouted, "Praise God!"

As he ran home, followed by his friends, Justus yelled over his shoulder, "Peter, we'll get our tools and come back to fix your roof."

OPEN YOUR BIBLE

Read the original story

Read the story of Jesus healing the paralyzed man in Mark 2:1–12; Matthew 9:1–8; and Luke 5:17–26.

Compare Bible stories and verses

Read the story of the prodigal son in Luke 15:11–32. What does the father do when his son returns home? How is the story of the prodigal son like the story of Justus?

Answer some questions

1. Why is Justus more anxious to have his sins forgiven than to be healed?
2. Why are the Jewish leaders so angry at Jesus when He makes the radical announcement to Justus that his sins are forgiven?
3. Who alone can forgive sins? If Jesus can forgive sins, who is He?

Learn a Bible verse

" 'Which is easier: to say, "Your sins are forgiven," or to say, "Get up and walk"? But I want you to know that the Son of Man has authority on earth to forgive sins.' So he said to the paralyzed man, 'Get up, take your mat and go home' " (Matthew 9:5, 6).

Share Jesus with others

1. Research to see how houses were built in Jesus' time. Then build a small model of Peter's house. Use the model to tell the story of Justus to a friend.
2. Write the story of Justus as if you were a newspaper reporter. Be sure to answer the *w* questions—who, what, where, when, and why is this story important in modern times. Take close-up pictures of the model you created for activity 1. Then, ask someone to help you type the story or type it yourself. Submit your story and your picture to your church or school secretary, asking if it can be printed as an article in the next newsletter.
3. If you have chosen to be a follower of Jesus, you can claim the promise from Romans 8:1, "Therefore, there is now no condemnation for those who are in Christ Jesus." But it's easy to think about the past and worry about wrong choices. Read Philippians 3:13, 14 where Paul talks about forgetting the past and looking forward to the prize promised by Jesus. Write a six-word summary of the message of these two verses. Post it in places you'll see it to remind yourself that you, like Justus in this story, are forgiven.

Chapter 9

INTERRUPTED BY JOY

Abby knelt by her son's bed. "Oh, God, please heal my son. He is all I have left, and he is so sick. He breathes slowly as if it is very painful. The doctor gave up. You are all I have left," she prayed.

Benjamin groaned. Abby dampened a cloth with cool water and wiped his face. Again, she prayed, "Dear Lord, I heard about Jesus from Nazareth who makes people well. I am not strong; I can't carry Benjamin to him. But I think He could heal my son. Please heal Benjamin and make him well again."

"Hello," someone called at the door. Abby got up from her knees and went to the door. Leah, her closest friend, came in. "Abby, I heard some wonderful news. One of the men said he saw Jesus and His disciples in Capernaum the day before yesterday. They left the city walking in this direction. If Jesus comes here, He'd heal Benjamin," she said.

"Leah, Jesus needs to be here now. Benjamin is much worse. I'm afraid that he will die before Jesus can get here. It's a long walk from Capernaum to Nain," Abby told her friend. "Look, the sun will soon set. No one can walk on that mountain road in the dark. I'm afraid; I'm afraid that by morning it will be too late."

Abby and Leah sat by Benjamin's bed. Abby tried to give him a sip of water but he couldn't swallow. "Hello," a deep voice called.

"Come in," Abby called.

Joash, Leah's husband, came into the room. "How is Benjamin feeling?" he asked.

"He's getting worse every hour," Abby answered. "I've been praying and praying. I don't know how to help my son. If only Jesus were here," she sighed.

"Leah, you stay here with Abby tonight," Joash told his wife. "I'll bring you some bread and cheese. Abby needs some food and some water," he said as he walked out the door into the twilight.

When Joash returned with the food, Leah tried to get Abby to eat. "You must have some food. You must drink some water," she said.

Abby tried to eat, but she had no appetite. Leah held the cup for Abby to drink, and she had a few sips. Together the two women sat by Benjamin's bed. Sometimes they prayed. Sometimes they talked, remembering their friendship through the years. "Do you remember Amos's accident?" Abby asked. "Do you remember the bull and how he got out of his pen?"

"I'll never forget it," Leah said. "That bull tossed him—a strong man—like he was a little child. And you ran out into the field to where Amos lay on the ground even before the other men caught the bull. I thought the bull would kill you too."

"I loved Amos so much. He was a good husband, kind and never cross—even if I burned our dinner. His body was all broken by the bull. At least he didn't suffer a long time. But since then, I've had Benjamin. Now I will have no one."

"Have faith, Abby. Don't lose hope," Leah said.

Both women grew quiet and dozed off for a little while. Suddenly Abby's head dropped and she jerked, realizing that she had fallen asleep. She looked at Benjamin and saw that his breathing had stopped. She reached out and touched his hand.

"Touch Benjamin's hand. It's not hot anymore. The fever is gone, but he must be dead," she nudged her friend awake.

Leah touched Benjamin's hand too. She threw her arms around Abby who sobbed and sobbed. "Oh, God, why didn't You heal Benjamin?" she cried.

As the day dawned, the two women washed Benjamin's body and wrapped it in the linen cloths with spices that people of their day used to prepare a body for burial. They lit candles at his head and at his feet.

Leah hurried home to tell Joash that Benjamin had died. "Please get some men to prepare a grave for him. He must be buried near Amos, his father."

Women from the town came to cry loudly for Abby's dead son. Some men came with a bier or platform used to carry a dead body. They placed Benjamin's body on the bier. Many people from town came to comfort Abby and walk with her to the place to bury her son. Slowly the crowd of people walked with Abby and the men who carried the bier, and many were crying loudly to mourn for Benjamin. As they passed through the city gate, they met Jesus leading another group of people.

Jesus came forward, stopping the men who carried Benjamin's body. Jesus spoke to Abby. "Don't cry" (Luke 7:13), He said to her softly. She sniffled, trying to stop her tears, and thought, *If only He had come yesterday.*

Jesus touched the bier and said, "Young man, I say to you, get up!" (Luke 7:14).

Benjamin sat up and asked, "What happened?"

Everyone spoke at once, trying to explain. Jesus smiled at Benjamin and Abby. "My son, you died. They were carrying you to be buried."

Abby interrupted, "Jesus came and brought you back to life. He gave me back my son! Yesterday I prayed and prayed for God to heal you. Today He has done more than that—today He brought you back to life. He gave me back my son from the dead!"

The whole crowd began singing praises to God, "A great prophet has appeared among us. . . . God has come to help his people" (Luke 7:16). Soon everyone in the surrounding towns heard about Jesus raising a dead man back to life.

Abby and Benjamin went home, praising God. "Do you think Jesus is the Messiah?" Benjamin asked his mother.

"He must be," she answered. "No one else could bring someone back from the dead."

OPEN YOUR BIBLE

Read the original story

Read the story about Jesus bringing Benjamin back to life in Luke 7:11–17.

Compare Bible stories and verses

Read about other people that Jesus raised from the dead in Mark 5:21–43 and John 11:1–44. How are these stories the same and how are they different from the story about Benjamin?

Answer some questions

1. Why do you think Jesus chose to arrive in Nain at the beginning of a funeral?
2. How do you think Abby's faith in Jesus changed after her son was brought back to life?
3. What hope does Jesus' radical rescue of Benjamin give to you?

Learn a Bible verse

"I am the resurrection and the life. The one who believes in me will live, even though they die; and whoever lives by believing in me will never die" (John 11:25, 26).

Share Jesus with others

1. Use a Bible concordance to find resurrection promises. List the verses in your journal.
2. Create a flyer or poster on paper or on a computer with resurrection

promises from the Bible together with pictures and graphics that show the assurance we have in Jesus. Share the flyer or poster you created with friends and family.

3. Imagine that you are either Abby or Benjamin. Write in your journal about your experience and feelings on the day that Jesus interrupted the funeral.

Chapter 10

PEACE AFTER THE STORM

Some seed fell on the rocky soil and the tiny plants were burned by the sun because they didn't have a good root system. Some fell on the path where the birds snatched them up. Other seeds fell into the weeds where they were choked and didn't grow. But some seeds fell into good soil and the harvest was plentiful," Jesus explained.

Jacob knew all about planting seeds. His father was a farmer. Just the week before Jacob's father had assigned him the task of planting the east field and the seed had fallen just as Jesus described. Jacob didn't know too much about the kingdom of heaven but he knew about growing plants. *I want my heart to be like the good soil,* he thought.

Jacob took off his sandals and dug his toes into the warm sand at the beach. Jesus taught from a boat, launched a little way onto Lake Gennesaret so all the people could see him. The slap, slap, slap of the small waves hitting the boat accompanied the calm voice of Jesus. Jacob wanted to listen to Jesus every day.

Close to sunset, he saw Jesus say something to His disciples. Jesus waved goodbye to the people, and the wind picked up the sails, carrying the boat away from shore. *Not yet!* Jacob thought. *I want to hear more!*

"Jacob! Quickly, get into our boat. We'll follow Jesus!" called Jacob's father.

Jacob didn't have to be asked twice. He ran for their small fishing boat and unfurled the sails. His two brothers climbed in after him while their father grabbed the rudder. Other families followed in their own boats too.

Darkness settled in on the lake but the full moon made it easy to see the outline of Jesus' boat. Jacob's father steered their boat to follow. The smooth water made it a lovely evening for a sail. At least, it started out as a lovely evening.

It didn't stay nice for long. Without warning, a cold wind picked up, blowing strongly from the west. Dark clouds blocked the moonlight. The waves grew bigger and bigger. The sails puffed up and carried their small boat forward at a dangerous speed.

"Take down the sails!" shouted Jacob's father above the screaming wind, as he struggled with the rudder. To Jacob's brothers he called, "Grab the oars!

Help me turn the boat so the water doesn't sink it!"

Thunder crashed and lightning filled the sky. The four of them struggled against the wind with all of their strength. But the wind grew stronger, and no matter how hard they rowed his brothers couldn't make any progress against the wind and waves. Jacob started throwing buckets of water back into the lake, but it was useless. The water filled their boat faster than he could throw it back into the lake.

Jacob glanced up quickly to see where they were. A flash of lightning showed him several of the boats had been tossed close to each other by the waves. Another flash and he saw the boat with Jesus in it. His disciples were working as hard as his family was to keep their boat under control. Another flash and crash, then he saw Jesus, but he wondered, *Wait, is that Jesus sleeping in the boat?*

Then Jacob barely heard the disciples shout above the wind, "Jesus, wake up! We're going to drown! Help us!"

When the lightning flashed again, Jacob watched Jesus hold onto the main mast and stand up. He didn't look frightened at all! Then Jacob heard Jesus' command, "Quiet! be still!" (Mark 4:39).

The wind stopped, the waves stopped. The lightning and thunder stopped. Within minutes, the water was smooth and the sky full of stars.

What kind of man is this Jesus that even the wind and the waves obey Him? Jacob thought.

"Why are you so afraid? Do you still have no faith?" Jesus asked His disciples (Mark 4:40).

Jacob thought to himself, *I was afraid because I thought we were about to drown. I didn't know You were so powerful, Jesus. I won't be afraid again.*

"Time to go home," said Jacob's father. "We'll tell our story because everyone needs to know about the power of Jesus."

OPEN YOUR BIBLE

Read the original story

Read Mark 4:35–41 to see how this story is told in the Bible. It is also told in Matthew 8:23–27 and Luke 8:22–25.

Compare Bible stories and verses

Another story about a time when people were afraid is in 2 Kings 6:8–23 when the servant of Elisha sees the Syrian army surrounding Samaria. How is this story similar to the story of Jesus calming the storm? How is it different?

Answer some questions

1. Why was Jesus able to sleep during the storm?
2. How do you think the disciples felt when Jesus asked them why they were afraid?
3. How has Jesus radically calmed a "storm" in your life?

Learn a Bible verse

"The disciples went and woke him, saying, 'Master, Master, we're going to drown!' He got up and rebuked the wind and the raging waters; the storm subsided, and all was calm" (Luke 8:24).

Share Jesus with others

1. Build a 3D pop-up picture that tells the story of Jesus calming the storm. Use this pop-up picture to share the story of Jesus calming the storm with someone you know.
2. Research about powerful hurricanes and typhoons. Share with your family how understanding the power of weather helps you understand the power of God better.
3. Make a video of three people telling their stories about how Jesus calmed a storm in their lives. Ask permission to share their stories with others. Add titles, background music, and combine the videos into a movie. Ask an adult to help you find an audience for your movie.

Chapter 11

"LEAVE US ALONE!"

Ethan! Ethan! Do you hear the storm?" asked Jason.

"I hear it and I see it!" the cousin groaned with a blanket over his head. "It's your turn to check on the pigs. Call me *only* if you need help!"

Jason grabbed his coat and left the cave all of the pig herders used when it was their turn to be on pig watch. He hated his job, but the pay helped his family, and the two thousand pigs owned by the people in the Gerasenes region needed someone to look out for them.

Once outside, Jason fought the wind to keep his coat closed. He simply wanted to look to see if the pigs were OK, but a dark fog hid everything. So, he stumbled toward the pig enclosure. The rock cliff rising behind the three sides of the pen would keep the pigs inside. But he carefully checked the rock barriers piled around the front of the pen. The pigs grunted and squealed at every boom of thunder. He could see them crowding together for comfort when the lightning flashed.

Good, he thought. *I can go back to the cave and try to sleep.*

The rain made his clothes heavy with water. He struggled up the hill against the wind. And then, halfway to the cave, Jason stopped moving and stared at everything around him. All within a minute's time the fog cleared, the wind calmed, the rain quit, and the stars shone. *How did that happen?* he wondered. *Storms usually ride out slowly with the wind.*

Jason glanced at the pigs, who were finally settling down to sleep. Then he surveyed the lake. The quiet water held a cluster of boats at the center.

Then he peered across the deep gully that separated the pigs from the tombs. He saw his Uncle Elon, wearing almost nothing, standing in front of the tomb where he sheltered. Uncle Elon gawked at the sky. *He looks as confused as me. Why did this storm disappear so quickly?*

Jason thanked God every day for the divide of the deep gully. He shuddered with fear at the thought of crossing paths with Uncle Elon. Jason remembered the stories telling how his Uncle Elon used to be a respected member of the family and the town, but now he roamed the tombs and caves on *his side* of the hill, ready to do harm to anyone who came near. The broken chains on his wrists and ankles proved the tales that nothing had been able to hold him back. No one wanted to be near the man with demons living inside of him.

Just thinking about the possibility made Jason run the rest of the way to the pig herder's cave. While Ethan snored loudly, Jason removed his coat and dried himself by the fire, still wondering about how the storm ended so quickly. Soon his head drooped. He woke up just long enough to drop onto his bed, pull his blanket around his shoulders, and adjust his pillow.

The next morning, when Ethan and Jason opened the gate to the pig pen, they heard terrifying screams. They turned around in time to see a group of men running for their boat. Uncle Elon tore down the hill toward them, roaring and shrieking almost louder than the thunder of the nighttime storm.

"Must be visitors to these parts," Jason laughed. "Landed their boat on the wrong side of the gully. Apparently, they aren't interested in meeting our local crazy!"

"Wait! Do you see that one Man standing still? He's not running. In fact, He's holding His hand up to stop Uncle Elon. If chaining him up doesn't stop him what's that going to do?" Ethan laughed as the pigs slowly made their way out of the pen.

"But He is stopping!" Jason exclaimed. "Look! Uncle Elon is kneeling down in front of the Man."

"What kind of Man is He? Even the demons obey Him!" Ethan exclaimed.

"Let's go closer so we can hear," suggested Jason.

After only a few steps they heard Uncle Elon scream, "What do you want with me, Jesus, Son of the Most High God? In God's name don't torture me!" (Mark 5:7).

"Come out of this man, you impure spirit!" Jesus commanded (Mark 5:8).

"What is your name?" Jesus asked.

"My name is Legion, . . . for we are many," they heard Uncle Elon growl (Mark 5:9). "Don't make us leave this area. Send us to the pigs instead."

"Go!" Jesus said.

Pigs, squealing and screaming, rushed through the open gate of their pen. Jason and Ethan jumped out of the way. As one group, the pigs stampeded down the hill, fell off the edge of the cliff, and drowned in the lake.

The boys took off running for town.

"The pigs have drowned! All of them!" shouted Ethan when they reached the town.

"A Man called Jesus sent Uncle Elon's demons into them! The pigs went crazy!" Jason reported.

"What are you saying?" the town elders cried.

"All two thousand pigs just ran off the cliff and drowned because of a Man named Jesus," repeated Ethan.

"What? What! We need to get that Man out of here! Who knows what He will do next!"

Then the townspeople followed after the boys as they raced back to Jesus, and when they found Him, they found Elon too. He sat in front of Jesus, clothed and calm.

"See the pigs!" shouted one. "In the water! They are all dead! The story is true."

"Are You the Man called Jesus?" a town elder asked.

"I am," replied Jesus.

"We heard about what happened here today and now we see all of our pigs drowned in the lake. Leave us alone!"

"Leave now! Leave now! Leave now! Leave now!" the townspeople chanted.

"We don't want You here," the elder stated loudly.

"I'll go," Jesus replied. He started walking toward the boat that held His disciples.

Elon followed. "Please, Jesus, let me go with You!"

"No, Elon. You have an important job here. Go home to your own people and tell them how much the Lord has done for you, and how He has had mercy on you" (see Mark 5:19).

"Yes, Lord, I'll do that. Thank You, Jesus! I owe my life to You." Elon hugged Jesus, then waved goodbye as the boat drifted away.

"Did you hear him, Ethan?" asked Jason.

"Who? Jesus?"

"No, Uncle Elon. He's a changed man. Jesus changed him," answered Jason. "Jesus calmed the storm in Uncle Elon. I believe He calmed the storm last night too."

"You think so?"

"Uncle Elon!" Jason called as he ran to the man. "Tell me your story! Tell me how Jesus changed you! I want Him to change me too!"

OPEN YOUR BIBLE

Read the original story

Find the story of Jesus' healing of the demoniac in Mark 5:1–20 and Luke 8:26–39.

Compare Bible stories and verses

Matthew tells his version of this story in Matthew 8:28–34. Why do you think there are differences?

Answer some questions

1. Why do you think the villagers cared more about their pigs than about Jesus?
2. What did the demoniac understand about Jesus' radical rescue mission that the townspeople missed?
3. Why did Jesus ask the demoniac to stay with his people and tell his story?

Learn a Bible verse

"Go home to your own people and tell them how much the Lord has done for you, and how he has had mercy on you" (Mark 5:19).

Share Jesus with others

1. In your journal, make a list of stories in the Bible that illustrate how Jesus is stronger than Satan.
2. The people in this story are focused on their pigs and they send Jesus away. Is there anything in your life that causes you to send Jesus away? Ask Jesus to help you keep your focus on Him.
3. First John 3:18 says, "Dear children, let us not love with words or speech but with actions and in truth." When Jesus changes hearts, people can love others. Ask Jesus to give you ideas of loving and truthful "actions" you can do to share with others how He has changed your heart. Write the ideas in your journal and pick some to put into "action."

Chapter 12

TWO BY TWO

"See those three rocks over there?" Nathanael asked Philip as they walked down the road.

"Yeah. What about them?" replied Philip.

"I can throw this pebble and hit the small one on the left side."

"Sure, you can," Philip was not impressed.

"Watch me!" his friend boasted. Nathanael took aim, threw the pebble, and missed.

"I didn't think you could do it!" chided Philip.

"Wait! I'm going to try again." Nathanael took aim, and threw a second pebble.

Philip and Nathanael watched the pebble hit the smallest rock and land on the ground.

"Hey! That's pretty good! With practice your aim could get even better," complimented Philip.

"Thanks!"

Nathanael and Philip continued walking. "Philip, why do you think Jesus sent us out to talk to people in the villages?"

"Jesus sent us out two by two so we could practice telling others about Him. He also told us to go into the villages and heal the sick," Philip answered.

"I never thought of it that way. Are you saying you think Jesus trusts us to tell people the kingdom of God is near to them?"

"Exactly. He trusts us to help Him with His mission. Now we need to practice trusting God to help us," said Philip.

The sun baked the road where Philip and Nathanael traveled. They walked without speaking for several minutes. When a palm tree offered shade at the top of the hill, Philip and Nathanael stopped to rest. Looking into the valley below they saw a small village.

"I think we just found our first place to practice," said Nathanael. "I'm a little nervous."

"Me too," said Philip, "but remember Jesus told us to stay in the village only if they welcome us. If they don't, we clean the dust of the streets off our sandals and leave."

"Right. We see if there is someone who will let us stay at their house, we stay with them, and eat the food they offer us," listed Nathanael.

"And bless the household that gives us shelter," added Philip. "Nathanael?"

"Yes?"

"Will you pray for us before we go into the village? We've tried to do things on our own before and it doesn't go well. Before we do anything, we need to ask God to help us."

"Yes, I'll pray. Father, You know we want the people in this village to believe in You and in Your Son, Jesus, as the Messiah. Help us as we work in Jesus' name," prayed Nathanael.

"I don't feel quite so nervous now."

"I actually feel a little hungry—I hope someone will take us in so we can eat supper tonight. Let's go!" With that Nathanael took off running. "I'm going to beat you to the village gates!"

Philip started running after him and cried, "Better run fast!"

Laughing and out of breath they reached the village gate at the same time.

"Why are you laughing?" asked an old beggar. "And why are you so out of breath? Are you two the reason I heard pounding footsteps coming down the road?"

"Yes, that was us," said Philip.

"Were you running because you were in danger?"

"No real danger. Only the danger of losing the footrace." Nathanael took a closer look at the old man. "Sir, what is your name?"

"My name is Abdiel."

"Abdiel, would you like to be cured of your blindness?" he asked.

"I have prayed for my sight to return for more than twenty years, but God has always answered my prayer with a no."

"Or maybe it was a not yet," Philip replied. Philip put his hands on the blind man's eyes, just as he had seen Jesus do many times. "In the name of Jesus Christ of Nazareth, your blindness is gone."

Abdiel opened his eyes. He looked at Philip and then at Nathanael. Then he threw down his walking stick and ran through the gate. "I can see! Everyone!" he yelled. "Look at me! I can see!"

The others near the village gates turned to look. They knew Abdiel. He lived with his sister's family and begged at the village gate to help with expenses. The villagers would often stop to share a piece of news and a coin or two.

"Abdiel! What are you saying?" several asked.

"These men healed me in the name of Jesus of Nazareth. Now I can see!"

"Please stay for a few days in our village and tell us more about Jesus of Nazareth," the villagers begged Philip and Nathanael.

"And you can stay at my sister's house! She is the best cook in the whole village," proclaimed Abdiel. "I'll run ahead and tell her to make extra food for supper."

Philip and Nathanael smiled.

When they left the village at the end of the week, every villager who needed help had been healed. They looked forward to a visit from Jesus.

"May God go with you and carry you on your mission with peace," the villagers gave their blessing to Philip and Nathanael. The two men walked out of the village gates as everyone waved and called out their goodbyes.

"Philip?"

"Yes, Nathanael?"

"God worked miracles through us in that village."

"We can trust Him," answered Philip.

Philip and Nathanael traveled to several villages before returning to Jesus. They wondered if the other disciples also had stories to tell.

"Wait until you hear the news!" they shouted a few days later when they saw Jesus and their friends in the distance.

"Wait until you hear *our* news!" several of the disciples called back to them.

"I want to hear *all* of your stories!" Jesus grinned.

What a celebration they had sharing how God had worked miracles through the trusting disciples of Jesus!

OPEN YOUR BIBLE

Read the original story

Read the story about Jesus sending out the twelve disciples in pairs in Matthew 10:1–42; Mark 6:6–12; and Luke 9:1–6. Read a similar story about a time Jesus sent out seventy-two disciples in Luke 10:1–23.

Compare Bible stories and verses

Read about the Great Commission Jesus gave His disciples right before He went back to heaven in Matthew 28:16–20 and Acts 1:1–8. How are these stories the same and how are they different compared to the story of Jesus sending out His disciples in twos?

Answer some questions

1. What did Jesus ask Nathanael, Philip, and all of His disciples to do? Why do you think He told them to take no money or food with them?
2. What happened in the village that made the people interested in listening to Nathanael and Philip?

3. How did the disciples sharing Jesus' message fit in with God's plan to radically rescue people?

Learn a Bible verse

"Therefore go and make disciples of all nations, baptizing them in the name of the Father and of the Son and of the Holy Spirit, and teaching them to obey everything I have commanded you. And surely I am with you always, to the very end of the age" (Matthew 28:19, 20).

Share Jesus with others

1. If it's near Christmas, plan with your family to go caroling to your neighbors. Sing songs about Jesus to share the good news of Him coming to earth to radically rescue people from sin.
2. If it's near Easter, deliver a flower or small plant and a card that tells the story of Jesus' radical rescue plan to your neighbors.
3. If it's near your country's independence day, deliver decorated cards to your neighbors with John 8:36 printed on them: "So if [Jesus] sets you free, you will be free indeed." Include a celebration message about being thankful for the gift of freedom enjoyed by your country and the gift of freedom from sin offered by Jesus.

Chapter 13

WALKING ON THE WATER

Peter, you look tired. Let me row for a while," Andrew offered. Andrew and Peter traded places in the boat.

"What a strange day," Peter sighed.

"The day began so well. I felt so close to Jesus," said Philip. "He healed so many people, and then after all the stories He told, He asked us to find food for over five thousand people!"

"That little boy, what was his name? He brought Jesus his lunch," said James.

"Jared, Jared was his name," Andrew added.

"Jesus made one child's lunch enough to feed the whole crowd," said John. "Jesus always surprises me. I never know what He will do next."

The rowers were working harder now. The wind blew against them so they seemed to make no progress in crossing the Sea of Galilee.

"Where is Jesus now? We need Him!" said John.

"I just don't understand," said Judas. "The people wanted to make Him King. We've been waiting and waiting to have Jesus made King. Why did He send us out here on the lake to go back to Capernaum?"

"Jesus would be the most wonderful King imaginable," added Thomas. "We would have no sick people. He would chase the Romans out of our country. Everyone would have plenty to eat. It would be like heaven on earth. Long live King Jesus!"

"Why doesn't Jesus want to be King?" asked Philip.

"I think He wants to heal people's hearts and teach them to be friends with God," John said. "He wants to solve deeper problems than just getting rid of the Romans."

The waves grew higher. The wind blew harder. Those fishermen who knew that lake so well, who had fished its waters for years, grew afraid for their lives.

Those twelve men in the boat on the lake prayed and prayed for help. "We need Jesus! We need Jesus now!" each one cried.

The sky became a little lighter in the east as the stars faded. "We've been out here on the lake, rowing all night," said Peter. "I'm exhausted."

Someone noticed a figure moving toward them across the lake. "Wh– what's that?" asked Andrew.

"May, maybe it's a ghost," Thomas whispered.

"I wish Jesus were here," John whispered.

A voice came across the water. "Take courage! It is I. Don't be afraid" (Matthew 14:27). It was Jesus' voice. All the disciples' fear turned to joy. Here was Jesus when they needed Him most.

"Lord, if it's you," Peter called, "tell me to come to you on the water" (Matthew 14:28).

"Come," Jesus answered (Matthew 14:29).

Peter climbed over the side of the boat and started walking on the water toward Jesus. Looking at Jesus, he continued walking. *Wow! This is fun! I'm actually walking on the water. Is Andrew, my brother, watching? Are James and John, my fishing buddies, watching?* Peter turned to look back at the boat. Then a big wave came up, and he could no longer see Jesus. Peter started to sink in the water. No longer was walking on the water fun—it was frightening! "Lord, save me," he yelled (Matthew 14:30).

Immediately, Jesus took Peter's hand and pulled him up. "Keep your eyes on Me, Peter. I won't let you drown," Jesus said. Together they walked on the water to the boat. Then, as Peter and Jesus climbed into the boat, the wind and the waves calmed. All the disciples turned to Jesus, saying, "Truly you are the Son of God," and they worshiped Him (Matthew 14:33).

The men kept rowing, but now it was easy. Very quickly they arrived in Capernaum.

When people saw that Jesus was back in their city, they hurried to bring people who needed healing to Him. Some were healed just by touching the hem of His robe!

Others in the crowd had seen the disciples leave the other side of the lake without Jesus. Yet now He arrived with the disciples, so they asked, "How did You get here? You weren't with the disciples when they left the place where You fed us yesterday." But Jesus did not answer them.

"You haven't come to see the healings I'm doing," Jesus said. "You've come because you had plenty to eat yesterday. I'll give you food to prepare you for eternal life."

"Do a sign so we may believe You," some in the crowd said. "Our ancestors ate manna that Moses gave them in the wilderness for forty years."

Philip and Andrew talked quietly to each other. "How can the crowd ask for a sign when Jesus fed thousands only yesterday?" asked Andrew.

"Yes, and they've seen Him heal many sick people both yesterday and today," Philip said. "He's already given them many signs."

"Moses did not give our fathers the manna; it was a gift from My heavenly Father. The bread of God is He who comes down from heaven and gives life to the world," Jesus answered.

"Please give us some of that bread," men in the group said.

"I am the bread of life," Jesus told them (John 6:35). "The person who comes to Me will never be hungry or thirsty. My Father sent Me from heaven because everyone who believes in Me will have eternal life."

Many in the crowd started grumbling. "How can Jesus say that He is the bread that came from heaven? We know His father and His mother and many of us saw Him grow up in Nazareth."

"Don't grumble among yourselves. Those who come to Me are led by My Father and His Spirit. Your ancestors ate the manna in the wilderness, but they died. I am the living bread that came down from heaven. Whoever eats this bread will live forever. This bread is My flesh which I will give to save My people" (see John 6:49–51), Jesus said.

The crowd's grumbling turned into an argument. "How can this man give us His flesh to eat? We are not cannibals. We don't eat people!" (see John 6:52).

"Whoever eats my flesh and drinks my blood has eternal life, and I will raise them up at the last day," Jesus told them (John 6:54).

"We don't understand what You are teaching," said many of His followers.

Jesus answered, "Are you offended by My words? The words I speak to you are full of life."

Many in the crowd turned and walked away from Jesus. They never followed Him again. Jesus turned to His twelve disciples. "Will you go away too?" He asked them.

Peter answered, "Lord, to whom shall we go? You have the words of eternal life. We have come to believe and to know that you are the Holy One of God" (John 6:68, 69).

The others all agreed. "We believe that You are the promised Messiah. We know that You have come to us from God."

Jesus and His twelve disciples were sad that so many no longer followed Him. "I guess those who left wanted a Messiah who would give them food without work and who would free us from the Romans who govern us. You wouldn't be that kind of King," the disciples said as they talked over what had happened with Jesus. "Now they don't want You to have any part in their lives; and only yesterday they wanted You to be their King."

"Yes, you do understand," Jesus agreed with them.

OPEN YOUR BIBLE

Read the original story
Read the original Bible story as found in Matthew 14:22–36; Mark 6:45–56; and John 6:1–69.

Compare Bible stories and verses
Read the story of Jesus feeding another large crowd in Matthew 15:29–39. How is that story the same as this one and how is it different?

Answer some questions
1. Why did Jesus send the disciples across the lake?
2. Why were the disciples afraid when they saw Jesus walking on the water?
3. What radical ideas did Jesus share that made some of His followers decide to leave Him? Why did the twelve disciples decide to stay?

Learn a Bible verse
"For my Father's will is that everyone who looks to the Son and believes in him shall have eternal life, and I will raise them up at the last day" (John 6:40).

Share Jesus with others
1. As long as Peter focused on Jesus he could walk on the water as Jesus did. When he looked away, he started to sink. Record in your journal a plan about how you can keep your focus on Jesus every day? Ask God to help you keep your plan.
2. Research about the Sea of Galilee. How big is the lake? In good weather, how long would it take to row across the lake? Write in your journal how what you know about the Sea of Galilee helps you understand more about Jesus?
3. Talk to a parent, pastor, or teacher about what Jesus meant when He said, "I am the bread of life." What does Jesus being the Bread of Life have to do with the people on earth being radically rescued?

Chapter 14

UNEXPECTED CHANGES

The setting sun had transformed the clouds into an artist's palette overflowing with purple, red, and orange hues when Jesus and His disciples arrived at the base of a mountain at the end of a full day's journey. They were tired, but Jesus wanted to climb the mountain, and He invited three of His disciples to join Him: Peter, James, and John. The other nine stayed behind. Peter, James, and John knew Jesus wanted to pray as He often did. They took the invitation to pray with Him seriously, so they climbed together.

"Can we rest a minute?" Peter asked halfway up. "I'm out of breath!"

The others were happy Peter had asked for the pause.

"Will you look at all those stars!" remarked James. "I see them more clearly up here."

"The moon is missing tonight. That helps too," added John.

"True. All I know is the sky is extra beautiful tonight," Peter said. "Remember this psalm?" Peter started them off and the others joined in after the first line.

"The heavens declare the glory of God;
the skies proclaim the work of his hands.
Day after day they pour forth speech;
night after night they reveal knowledge.
They have no speech, they use no words;
no sound is heard from them.
Yet their voice goes out into all the earth,
their words to the ends of the world" (Psalm 19:1–4).

The voices sank into the silence of the night while each of them gazed at the millions of stars and thought about the glory of God.

After a few minutes, Jesus asked, "Ready to continue?"

"Sure!" they all agreed.

At the top of one of the ridges, Jesus said, "This is far enough for tonight. I'm going to pray over there by that olive tree. Please stay here and pray."

The disciples watched Jesus make His way up the hill a little further to the tree. Then they started to pray. But the long day of work and the steep mountain climb had their effects on Peter, James, and John. Soon they fell into a peaceful slumber.

Without warning, a blazing light interrupted their snoozing. It was brighter and more intense than anything they had ever seen, and at the center stood Jesus—totally transformed by the power of God. When their eyes finally adjusted, they realized Jesus stood with Moses and Elijah. The disciples struggled to understand what they were seeing. They stared speechlessly at the scene.

Is this a dream? they wondered as the brilliant light chased away their groggy thoughts.

It was Peter who spoke first. "Master, it's a good thing we are here to see this! I have an idea! We could build three shelters on the mountain. One could be for You, another for Moses, and the last for Elijah!" Even though he was afraid, Peter felt satisfied and happy about his plan.

However, in the next instant, a cloud slowly swallowed up the scene along with James, John, and Peter. They trembled and fell down with their faces to the ground as a voice declared, "This is my Son, whom I love. Listen to him!" (Mark 9:7).

And then, the voice, the cloud, the light, Moses, and Elijah disappeared.

Jesus walked over to His friends. He tapped them on the shoulders and said, "It's OK. You don't have to be afraid. You can get up now."

James looked at John. John looked at Peter. Peter looked at James. "Was that my imagination?" Peter asked.

"Couldn't be," whispered James, "since all three of us saw and heard the same thing."

"The words we heard—they were the same words people heard at Jesus' baptism," John reminded them.

"We have witnessed something from heaven," stated James.

At sunrise, Jesus cheerfully asked, "Ready to go back down and join the others?"

Awed at being in the presence of God's Son, Peter, James, and John cautiously followed Jesus down the mountain. As they walked, He instructed them, "Don't tell the others what you saw last night until the Son of Man has risen from the dead."

What is that supposed to mean, they wondered.

A crowd of people waited for them at the base of the mountain.

"There He is! There's Jesus!" called someone.

"Take the boy to Jesus," shouted another.

"What's going on?" Jesus calmly asked as the crowd circled around.

A man stepped forward and fell at Jesus' feet. "Master, I asked Your disciples to help my son, but they couldn't. He has these seizures that make him fall into the fire or into water. The condition is going to kill him."

"How long has he had this problem?" inquired Jesus.

"Since he was a young child," the father answered. "Please, Jesus, heal my son if You can."

"If I can? Everything is possible if you believe."

"You can heal him. I know You can. Please help me with my doubt!" the father desperately begged.

"Bring the boy to Me."

A seizure overtook the boy as he was led to Jesus. He fell to the ground. His mouth foamed with saliva. The crowd watched in fear.

"Come out of the boy and never go into him again!" Jesus commanded.

The boy rolled violently on the ground, became stiff as a board, and then gave an agonized shriek. A minute later he lay still, his body limp.

"He's dead," someone murmured.

"It definitely looks like he's dead," another person agreed.

Jesus walked over to the boy. He took his hand and helped him stand.

"Here is your son," Jesus led the boy to his father.

"Thank You, Jesus! Thank You! You healed my son!" praised the boy's father. The father and son embraced and spun around in celebration. As they headed for home, the father could be seen alternately waving his arms, sharing about Jesus whenever they passed someone, and hugging his son.

"Did you see that?" Peter asked John and James.

"Yes! The boy is transformed. He's totally healed," exclaimed John.

"Two total transformations in twelve hours," mused James. "Only by the glory and power of God."

"Jesus, why couldn't we heal the boy?" the other disciples wanted to know.

"This type of situation takes a lot of prayer," Jesus answered. "Ask God for faith—the kind that moves mountains."

OPEN YOUR BIBLE

Read the original story

The story of the transfiguration and the boy being healed can be found in Matthew 17:1–21; Mark 9:1–29; and Luke 9:28–42.

Compare Bible stories and verses

Read about when Elijah was taken to heaven in a chariot of fire in 2 Kings 2:1–18. How does this help you understand the story of Elijah meeting with

Jesus on the top of the mountain? Ask your pastor, parent, or teacher to explain why Moses met with Jesus too.

Answer some questions

1. Why do you think Jesus chose Peter, James, and John to witness His visit with Moses and Elijah on the mountain top?
2. What radical information did Peter, James, and John learn about Jesus on the top of the mountain?
3. Who was changed, and how, when Jesus healed the boy?

Learn a Bible verse

After Jesus healed the boy, His disciples asked why they were unable to heal him. Memorize Jesus' answer to them: "Truly I tell you, if you have faith as small as a mustard seed, you can say to this mountain, 'Move from here to there,' and it will move. Nothing will be impossible for you" (Matthew 17:20).

Share Jesus with others

1. Research to find out how big a mustard seed is. Talk with a trusted adult about what it means to have faith the size of a mustard seed.
2. Do you ever doubt that Jesus can or will do what He promises in the Bible? In this story, the father of the boy cried out to Jesus, "I do believe; help me overcome my unbelief" (Mark 9:24)! Jesus healed his son. The next time you have doubts, pray this same prayer. Write in your journal to record what happens in your thinking and in your heart.
3. Make a list of physical items that change when they are heated or chilled. How has Jesus changed something in your life? Use one of the items on your list to create a parable or word picture that helps a friend understand how Jesus has changed you.

Chapter 15

EYES COVERED IN MUD

"Excuse me, can you help me? Is this the road to the Pool of Siloam?" Kenan asked the man he heard talking.

"Yes, this is it. Be careful, though. There are lots of steps on the way down to the pool."

"Don't worry, I have my walking stick with me. It helps me find my way," Kenan answered.

"You'll be fine then. By the way, do you know you have mud all over your eyes?"

"Yes, I know. That's why I'm headed to the pool—to wash it off. Thanks for your help!" he replied and then headed down the road.

It took about thirty minutes of cautious walking, and going down countless steps, until Kenan heard the sound of the water. People passed by without greeting him, but that's something he'd gotten used to. They acted like they were invisible because Kenan couldn't see them, and they made a wide path around him.

Kenan had been to the Pool of Siloam last year with his parents, so when he felt the pillars at the entrance he knew it was only a short distance to the water. After counting the first set of stairs going down, then walking slowly across the landing, he found the second stairway and continued down until his feet felt the water.

Next, he set his walking stick on one of the steps while he bent over and splashed water on his face. The mud was hard to wash off where it had started to dry but he kept at it.

"Go, wash in the Pool of Siloam," Jesus had told him (John 9:7). That's why Kenan was there, though he wasn't sure what the result would be.

When all of the washing finally unsealed his eyes, he opened them and saw things for the first time. Water! That's what it looks like! Those must be trees! How tall they grow. Now I can hear and *see* the birds—they float in the air! The sky! That's what blue looks like!

"I can see!" Kenan shouted to anyone who was listening. However, he didn't stay to figure out who noticed. "I can see! I can see!" he kept shouting while hurrying back toward the temple. Every few steps, he would slowly turn around, trying to absorb everything he was seeing for the first time in his life.

"I can see!" Kenan called when he arrived in his neighborhood.

"Is that Kenan?" one woman asked.

"No, it can't be. Kenan is blind and he always sits in the same spot begging," her friend answered.

"It's me!" Kenan called, but they didn't hear.

"Hey, isn't that Kenan?" another asked.

"No, it must be someone who just looks like Kenan," the voice belonged to his cousin, Obed.

"Obed! It's me! It's me, Kenan! I can see! Jesus healed me."

Obed's eyes widened as he looked at Kenan. "Hey, everyone! Look at Kenan! He's not blind anymore!" called Obed.

A crowd started to gather. Neighbors and friends came out of their houses. Someone ran to get his parents.

"How is it that you can see?" asked Obed.

"About two hours ago a Man named Jesus came up to me, made some mud, and put it on my eyes. He told me to go wash in the Pool of Siloam. As soon as I washed off the mud, I could see!"

"A miracle! A miracle!" The voices of Kenan's parents echoed through the crowd, and he ran to hug them.

"Where is Jesus now?" they asked.

"I don't know, I wanted to thank Him but I don't know where to find Him."

"We need to take you to the temple leaders! They will want to know about this!" exclaimed Obed.

"Yes, let's go! A miracle in Israel! Jesus is the Messiah!" With that, the men led the way to the Pharisees and Kenan followed.

As Kenan stood in front of the Pharisees, they asked, "What happened? How did you get your sight?"

"Well," he replied, "I was born blind. Today, a man named Jesus put mud on my eyes and told me to go wash in the Pool of Siloam. Now I can see."

Since it was the Sabbath, they said, "Jesus most certainly can't be from God. He breaks the Sabbath."

But some of the Pharisees asked, "How can a sinner perform such signs?" (John 9:16).

Next, they turned to Kenan, "What do you say? You are the one who was blind. What do you think about this Man?"

That was an easy question to answer. "He is a prophet," Kenan replied (John 9:17).

"How do we know for sure that you have been blind since you were born?

Maybe you are making up this story. Summon his parents. We'll get to the bottom of this."

When Kenan's parents walked into the room, his mom's eyes never left the floor and his dad was trembling.

"Is this your son?" they questioned. "Is this the one you say was born blind? How is it that now he can see?" (John 9:19).

"Yes, this is our son, Kenan. He was born blind and has never been able to see anything until today. How he can now see, we don't know. He's old enough to answer for himself so ask him," Kenan's father stated. His voice was shaky because he was scared of being thrown out of the temple.

The Pharisees started asking more questions, "Jesus broke the Sabbath when He told you to wash on the Sabbath, so we know He's a sinner. Kenan, it's time to tell the truth. What really happened?"

Kenan discovered that his experience of being healed by Jesus had caused him to lose any fear of the Pharisees. He had nothing to hide, only wonderful news to share, and so he exclaimed, "Whether he is a sinner or not, I don't know. One thing I do know. I was blind but now I see!" (John 9:25).

"What did Jesus do to you? How did Jesus give you sight?" they asked again.

"I told you the whole story before. Why are you asking again? Do you want more information so you can become a disciple of Jesus too?" Kenan answered.

In their anger they replied with insults. They told Kenan that he could follow Jesus, but they followed Moses.

Truth be told, yes, Kenan wanted to be Jesus' disciple. But first, he had to find Him.

The Pharisees argued, "We know that God spoke to Moses, but as for this fellow, we don't even know where he comes from" (John 9:29).

"Now that is remarkable!" Kenan responded, "You don't know where he comes from, yet he opened my eyes. We know that God does not listen to sinners. He listens to the godly person who does his will. Nobody has ever heard of opening the eyes of a man born blind. If this man were not from God, he could do nothing" (John 9:30–33).

This statement made the Pharisees angrier than before, and they kicked Kenan out of the temple.

As he walked toward his home, a Man stopped him and asked, "Do you believe in the Son of Man?" (John 9:35).

"I don't know who He is. Can you show Him to me?" Kenan asked.

"It's Me," Jesus answered.

I knew *His voice sounded familiar!* Kenan thought to himself. Without any hesitation he threw himself down at His feet. "Jesus! I believe!"

OPEN YOUR BIBLE

Read the original story
Find the story of the man who was born blind in John 9.

Compare Bible stories and verses
Read two other stories about blind men Jesus healed. The first is a man who was in Bethsaida and that story is found in Mark 8:22–25. The second is about the healing of blind Bartimaeus in Mark 10:46–52. How are these stories the same and how are they different from the man who washed his eyes in the Pool of Siloam?

Answer some questions
1. According to the words in John 9:1–7, why did Jesus heal the blind man? Why was this a radical idea to the disciples?
2. Why did the temple leaders struggle to believe Jesus was from God?
3. Why do you think it was easy for Kenan to believe that Jesus was the promised Messiah?

Learn a Bible verse
In Revelation 21:3, 4, John describes the new earth, the ultimate destination of the people Jesus radically rescues from sin. Store this hope-filled promise in your memory: "And I heard a loud voice from the throne saying, 'Look! God's dwelling place is now among the people, and he will dwell with them. They will be his people, and God himself will be with them and be their God. "He will wipe every tear from their eyes. There will be no more death" or mourning or crying or pain, for the old order of things has passed away.' "

Share Jesus with others
1. Read about dogs who help blind people. Create a poster to explain how the dogs are trained to help their masters "see." What connections can you make between what the dogs do and how God helps us see? Share your poster at church or at school.
2. Imagine you are Kenan's mother and you are telling your story at the village well the morning after your son has been healed. What will you tell your friends about Kenan and about being called in to talk with the temple leaders? Will you tell them you believe Jesus is the Messiah? Why or why not? Write or act out your story to share with your friends or family.

3. Read Revelation 3:17, 18. Why is Jesus telling the church of Laodicea that they are blind? Discuss what this kind of blindness means with a pastor, teacher, or parent. Then make a list in your journal of things it's easy to be blind to and ask God to help you see what He wants you to see.

Chapter 16

JESUS IS OUR GUEST

"Hello, hello," someone called at the door. Martha went to the door to find the neighbor boy, David.

"Hello, David," she said. "What can I do for you?"

"Here, Martha. This is from your brother, Lazarus," David said, handing Martha a message.

"Thank you, David," she said and closed the door.

Martha quickly read the message, then she called, "Mary, Mary, come here quickly."

Mary came and asked, "What is it, Martha?"

"David brought a message from Lazarus. Here, read it," she told her sister.

Mary read the message aloud, "Martha and Mary, fix a good dinner with lots of food. I've invited Jesus and His disciples to have dinner with us tonight."

"Jesus? Jesus is coming to have dinner at our house? Amazing! What can we fix that will be good enough for Jesus?" Martha asked.

"How many disciples does He have? How much food do we need to make?" asked Mary.

"I've heard that He has twelve disciples. With you, me, and Lazarus we'll be sixteen people. Mary, go to the market and buy some fish. The people from around the Sea of Galilee will like fish. The bread we baked this morning won't be enough so get some at the bakery. I'll start some lentil stew," Martha instructed Mary.

Mary found the market basket and some money and went shopping. Martha started peeling onions for the lentil stew. *Jesus is coming to our house. We must have everything really special for Him. Let's see. How can we make the dinner special? Once the stew is started, I'll pick some roses from the garden to put on the table.*

Mary walked quickly to the market. People stood in little groups, talking excitedly. She stopped to listen as a tall bearded man said, "I heard Jesus telling everyone to be fair to their workers."

Another said, "His face is so kind, and His words make so much sense. I could listen to Him all day."

Suddenly, Mary remembered her errand and went to the fish booth, "What kind of fish do you have today?" she asked.

"Here is some fish, fresh from the Sea of Galilee," the vendor answered.

"Give me enough for twenty people," she told the man, handing him some money.

I will get some fruit too. Martha will like that, I hope that Jesus will too. I'd love to listen to the people talking about Jesus, but Martha will be fretting about getting everything ready. I'd better go help her.

When Mary got home, Martha had the stew cooking. "Mary, please sweep the floor. Then put a clean cloth on the table along with the roses I picked. We also need to get some cool water from the well for our guests to drink," Martha said.

"Yes, Martha. I'll sweep the floor, fix the table, and get some water from the well," Mary was still thinking about the people she had heard talking about Jesus at the market. "Martha, the people at the market were talking about Jesus and the stories He told. I would have liked to stay and listen, but I knew that you'd be worried about the dinner."

"Mary, please tell me about what Jesus said after we have dinner ready," Martha said as she started chopping the fish. "Do you think that we'll be ready on time? Will Jesus like the food?"

"Martha, you're known for being the best cook in town. Everything will be fine. Did you see that I got some fruit in addition to the fish?" Mary asked softly.

Soon the floor was clean, the table was set—including the vase of roses—and the stew and fish were cooking.

* * * * *

Before long, Lazarus brought the men into the house. "Martha, Mary, I want you to meet Jesus and His disciples."

"It smells so good in here," Jesus told the women. "I love the smell of delicious food."

Jesus sat down on a bench in the other room while His disciples sat around on the floor. He told them the meaning of the parables He had told the crowd that afternoon, Mary wanted to hear too. She forgot about the dinner and slipped quietly into a corner where she could sit and listen to Jesus. The men didn't notice her but Jesus smiled at her. She remembered that sometimes rabbis let women sit at their feet to listen with their disciples. Mary had memorized the Scriptures whenever she could. She especially loved the passages in Isaiah that told about the coming Messiah.

After a few minutes, Martha came into the room, and exclaimed, "Lord, don't you care that my sister has left me to do the work by myself? Tell her to help me!" (Luke 10:40).

"Martha, Martha," the Lord responded, "You are worried and upset about many things, but few things are needed—or indeed only one. Mary has chosen what is better, and it will not be taken away from her" (Luke 10:41, 42).

* * * * *

Soon Martha called the group to the table, and invited Jesus to bless the food.

"Let's thank God for the food, and eat," Jesus said. "Thank You, Father, for this good food. Thank You for giving us everything that we need."

"This fish is really good. It tastes like it came from the Sea of Galilee," one disciple said.

"The lentil stew is seasoned so nicely. Whenever I eat stew, I think about Jacob and Esau," said another.

"I love the cool water. I was so thirsty," said another.

Jesus turned to Martha and said, "Thank you for making us this delicious meal."

When they were done eating, the sisters hurriedly put away the leftovers and cleaned up the kitchen. "Martha, you must come listen to Jesus too. You will love listening to Him just as I do," Mary said.

Their work was quickly finished. Mary sat as near Jesus as she could so that she would not miss one word that He said. Martha listened carefully too.

* * * * *

Later, after the men were gone, Martha said, "Mary, now I know why you wanted to listen to Jesus. He explains the Scriptures like no one else I ever heard."

"Now, my sisters, you know why I invited Him to come to our house," Lazarus added.

"Please ask Him to be our guest again. We have so much to learn. Lazarus, do you think that He could be the Promised Messiah?" asked Mary.

"I pray that He is the Promised One," Lazarus responded.

OPEN YOUR BIBLE

Read the original story
Read the story of Mary and Martha in Luke 10:38–42.

Compare Bible stories and verses
Read another story about hospitality in 2 Kings 4:8–37. How is this story like the story of Martha and Mary? And, how is it different?

Answer some questions

1. Who understands the importance of Jesus' radical rescue mission more—Mary or Martha?
2. How can you create the right balance between sitting at Jesus' feet and being practical?
3. How can Jesus be a guest in your home?

Learn a Bible verse
"But seek first his kingdom and his righteousness, and all these things will be given to you as well" (Matthew 6:33).

Share Jesus with others

1. Ask your parent if you may plan a meal for a special guest. Plan dishes that you can prepare ahead so that you will have time to visit with the guest. If possible, actually invite the guest and prepare the meal. After your guest has gone home, discuss with your parent how your plan worked and what changes you might make for another dinner party. Did you make time to talk with your guest?
2. Talk to a parent or a teacher about ways to spend time with Jesus. Try some of them out and write about them in your journal.
3. Think of someone you know who has a big workload. What tasks can you help with so they have more time to spend with Jesus and with their family?

Chapter 17

CATCHING A COIN

"You don't know what you're talking about," James insisted. "I'm going to be the officer next to Jesus in His new kingdom. You just wait and see."

"No, I'll be the officer next to Jesus," Judas said. "You guys are just a bunch of uneducated fishermen. Jesus sees *my* talent."

"You might be the treasurer, but you'll never be prime minister. Did you see who Jesus took up the mountain with Him the other night? It was Peter, James, and me," John chimed in.

"John's right. We're the ones Jesus *really* trusts," Peter joined the argument.

The disciples were walking back to Capernaum with Jesus, but He had gone on ahead of them, seeming not to notice the argument. As they came into town, the disciples saw the temple tax collector's table set up near the street. "This must be the day to pay the temple tax," James observed.

Each year, every Jewish man was expected to pay a tax for the temple to buy the supplies needed in its services. It was paid with a Greek coin worth two drachmas so it was called the *didrachma.*

Noticing Peter, who was known as one of Jesus' disciples, the tax collector approached to ask him a question. "Does your Master pay the temple tax?"

Peter, thinking that he was defending Jesus' loyalty to the temple, immediately said, "Yes."

As they walked on, one of the others said, "You know, Peter, a prophet doesn't have to pay the temple tax."

"Oh, you mean, by saying yes, Peter may have denied that Jesus is a prophet?" asked another.

For a moment, Peter was unusually quiet, "Maybe the tax collector was told by one of the leaders who are always criticizing Jesus to trick me with his question."

"That's probably true," the others agreed.

Peter seemed sad. He really loved Jesus and never wanted to make Him trouble.

When they reached the house where they were staying, Peter went inside and found Jesus waiting for him. "Peter, tell Me what you think. When kings collect taxes, do they collect them from their own children or from others?" Jesus asked.

"From others," Peter answered.

"Then the kings' children don't have to pay," Jesus said. "We don't want to cause trouble so we will pay the tax. Peter, take your fishing line, go down to the lake. The first fish you catch will have a coin in its mouth. Use that coin to pay the tax for you and for Me."

"Yes, Master. I will do it," Peter said.

Peter found his fishing line, adjusted the hook, and walked to the lake. *Jesus always surprises me. How did He know that the tax collector had asked me about His paying the temple tax? I've caught fish all my life; and never have I caught one with money in its mouth. This should be interesting.*

Peter walked to a place where a large rock projected out into the water. He sat on the rock and threw the hook and line into the water, holding on to one end. The sunshine felt warm on his back and he thought, *This is why I like fishing.*

After a few minutes, he felt a tug on the line. *Maybe this is the fish Jesus told me about.* Peter pulled in the line, eager to check the fish that hung from the hook. He expertly unhooked the fish and opened its mouth. Just as Jesus had said, a coin was in its mouth—a coin worth four drachmas. Picking up the line, the fish, and the coin, Peter walked back to the house, humming a little tune.

"Jesus," he nearly shouted as he opened the door, "look, here's the fish and the coin, just like You said."

"We can have the fish for supper. Please take the coin to the tax collector," Jesus told him.

Peter walked back to where the tax collector had set up his table. "Here's the tax for Jesus and me," he said. "You'll never believe this story. I just have to tell you."

"What are you talking about, Peter?" the man asked.

"Jesus sent me fishing to get this coin," Peter said.

"What? Fishing to get a coin? Most people fish to get something to eat, not to get a coin," the tax collector scratched his head.

A crowd gathered around to listen to Peter and the tax collector.

"Jesus shouldn't have to pay the tax. He's a prophet. But He told me to take my line and hook to catch a fish. In the mouth of the fish, I would catch would be a coin to pay the tax for Him and for me. Here's the coin. It was in the fish's mouth, just like Jesus said. It's worth enough to pay the tax for both of us," Peter, who loved an audience, explained to the crowd.

Many shook their heads while others said, "Impossible! Jesus is amazing!" as Peter walked back to the house to fix the fish for supper.

OPEN YOUR BIBLE

Read the original story
Read the story about Peter's fishing trip in Matthew 17:24–27.

Compare Bible stories and verses
Read what Jesus says about paying taxes in Matthew 22:15–22. How is this story different from the story about the temple tax?

Answer some questions
1. What did Peter not understand about Jesus' radical rescue mission when he said that Jesus paid the temple tax?
2. Who didn't have to pay the temple tax?
3. What did paying the tax with a coin found in a fish's mouth show about Jesus?

Learn a Bible verse
"And my God will meet all your needs according to the riches of his glory in Christ Jesus" (Philippians 4:19).

Share Jesus with others
1. Make a drawing of Peter finding the coin in the fish's mouth. Share the story with someone you know.
2. Talk to your parent or another adult about how the church receives the money it needs to pay its bills. What kind of expenses does a church have?
3. Ask the pastor what you can do to help your church. Talk with your family about how to complete or help with some of the items on your pastor's list.

Chapter 18

A WEALTHY MAN WONDERS

"The inventory report is ready, master," said Uri. "We have counted everything that you own. Would you like to hear the total numbers or just the increases?"

"The increases would be fine. I already know I am rich, but I'd like to know how my riches grew last year," answered Nathan.

"Yes, sir. First, I'll tell you about the increases we counted in the animals you own. There are

- "158 sheep,
- "21 oxen,
- "94 pigeons,
- "18 donkeys,
- "47 goats,
- "10 horses, and
- "15 camels.

We were not able to count the fish in your personal ponds but we estimate the fish population has doubled since last year. Your animals are well fed and are multiplying quickly."

"This sounds wonderful, Uri. Thank you for organizing my servants to do such a careful job of managing the animals."

"Of course, Master Nathan. It is a privilege to work for you."

"What other increases does the inventory show?"

"We were just talking about your servants so I'll give you those numbers next. Your household has increased by seven field workers, eight household servants (including two new cooks), and five shepherds and animal caretakers. They all report that they are happy to be a part of your estate. They enjoy helping you take care of your land, your house, and your belongings."

"Excellent! What else?"

"Your wheat harvest saw an increase of two hundred bushels. The fruit orchards produced 710 more baskets of fruit compared to last year. The beekeepers collected fifty-nine extra jars of honey, and your vegetable gardens more than supplied your needs for gourmet meals and the food required to feed all of your servants. In addition, the villagers agree that your vegetable stall at the village market is, by far, the best place to shop for fresh produce."

"Fabulous! What do the numbers show for my silver and gold?"

"An increase of forty-two talents of silver and 183 gold coins. If I may say so, Master, you are most fortunate to have so many possessions at the young age of twenty-nine. Your barns are full and you don't need a single thing. Would you be willing to share with me the secret of your success?" asked Uri.

"Uri, my faithful servant, I believe it is because I have always worked hard to do what God wants me to do. Thanks to the faithful teaching of my parents, I have followed all of God's commandments from the time I was a young boy. I don't lie, I don't murder, I am faithful to my wife, I don't steal, and I took care of my parents as long as they were alive."

"I see," said Uri. "I can testify that you have loved your neighbor as you love yourself. I have seen you be kind over and over again."

"I didn't realize that you noticed," said Nathan.

"The most serious part of my job is understanding what makes you happy, Master Nathan. That means I pay attention to everything so I can learn how you would like for me to work for you."

"That's what makes you my trusted servant!" laughed Nathan.

"May I ask you one more question, Master Nathan?"

"Certainly. What would you like for me to tell you?"

"Master Nathan, you have all the possessions any man could want. Yet, sometimes I see you looking sad, or worried—or maybe distressed. I'm not exactly sure what I see. Is there something I can do to help you?"

"Uri, you are more than a trusted servant. You are a caring friend. You do notice everything. Let me see if I can explain what I have been thinking—I'm worried that maybe I haven't done enough."

"Done enough?"

"Maybe I haven't done enough to earn, to possess, or to obtain eternal life. Do you ever worry about that Uri?"

"Yes. I believe that every person must wrestle with that question in order to find peace. That's what I see, Master. You are not at peace!"

"That's right, Uri. I am not at peace, and I don't know where or how to find it."

"Have you heard about the Teacher named Jesus? I think He might be able to help you find your answer. I found out that He is traveling near our region in Judaea. Why don't you ask Him?"

"Do you think He would have time to talk to me? He's so popular. I understand there are always crowds surrounding Him."

"We can try! I'll get the stable workers to saddle two horses tomorrow morning. I'll have one of the other servants find out where Jesus will be, and then we can ride out to meet Him."

"I'll be ready early!" answered Nathan.

Uri smiled, "I will meet you in front of the main house."

Early the next morning, Uri sent out a servant to find Jesus. As soon as the servant returned with His location, Uri led two saddled horses to the main house. Master Nathan kept his promise and stood there, ready and waiting. The riders headed out to find Jesus.

"I've been thinking all night about how I will ask Jesus my question. How does this sound? 'Good Teacher, what must I do to inherit eternal life?' " (see Mark 10:17).

"Master Nathan, if the question comes from your heart, Jesus will listen," answered Uri.

Thirty minutes later, the two riders came upon a large group of people. From their vantage point on top of their horses, they could see Jesus at the front.

"There He is!" exclaimed Uri. "But He's waving goodbye to the people. He is getting ready to leave."

"It would not be safe to take the horses through this crowd, and I will never get to Him on foot. What should I do?" asked Nathan.

"Follow me!" Uri rode his horse along the edge of the throng. Nathan followed. When they reached the front of the group Uri suggested, "Master Nathan, if you dismount and give me the reins, then you can run to Jesus from here. I'll wait for you."

Uri's eyes followed his master as he wove his way toward Jesus. He saw his master reach Jesus and kneel down in front of Him. Uri recognized the love in Jesus' eyes as He spoke with Nathan. He saw the hope in Nathan's expression. Then he witnessed his master drop his head, turn away from Jesus, and walk sadly back toward the horses. Why?

Nathan did not look at Uri as he slowly reached for his horse's reins. He climbed into the saddle and pointed his horse toward home. Uri followed. He wisely waited for his master to speak.

About halfway home, Nathan said, "Jesus told me I needed to sell everything that I have and give to the poor."

"Oh?" answered Uri.

"I can't do that! Doesn't Jesus realize that I need to be able to take care of myself? Does He realize how much I own? If I sell everything that I have and give it away to the poor, that leaves me with nothing and leaves me poor!"

"Yes, but—" Uri tried to speak.

"Isn't it good enough that I have lived up to God's commandments all of my life? Isn't it good enough that I have loved my neighbors like myself?"

"Master, you—"

"If I am poor, who is going to take care of me? What is He asking me to do? Rely on God for everything? Rely on God's gift for eternal life?"

"That might be His point, sir."

"Well, I think that's crazy! If that's what it takes to earn eternal life then maybe it's just not for me."

The two rode the rest of the way home in silence. Nathan dismounted and left his horse in front of the house. With slumped shoulders and his eyes on the ground, he walked to the front door.

Uri led the horses back to the stable and prayed, "Lord God in heaven, someday, may my master understand that he can trust You with his life."

OPEN YOUR BIBLE

Read the original story

Read the story of the rich young ruler in Matthew 19:16–30. It can also be found in Mark 10:17–31 and Luke 18:18–30.

Compare Bible stories and verses

Compare the story of the rich young ruler to a parable in Luke 12:16–21 where Jesus told about a man who wanted to build more barns to store his huge harvest. How is this story the same and how is this story different?

Answer some questions

1. What did Jesus tell Nathan about how to be radically rescued and why did that make them both sad?
2. Why were the disciples sad when Jesus told them it is difficult for someone who is rich to enter heaven?
3. When do you think it's hard to trust Jesus?

Learn a Bible verse

"Jesus looked at them and said, 'With man this is impossible, but with God all things are possible' " (Matthew 19:26).

Share Jesus with others

1. Create people from clay, paper, or other building materials you have

available and make a stop-motion animation video of this story by taking multiple pictures of the figures as they move through the story. Consider adding narration and sound effects to the video once the animation is completed. Share your video.

2. Jesus told His disciples that it was easier for a camel to go through the eye of a needle than for a rich man to be saved. Research to find out what this statement means.
3. Did Nathan ever change his mind and sell everything to give it to the poor? The Bible doesn't say. Consider the possibility and write a story that gives details about when Nathan decides to follow what Jesus said. Share your story.

Chapter 19

WHO IS THE GREATEST?

"I'll be the most important of Jesus' officers in His new kingdom," Judas said, as the disciples walked along the dusty road.

"Judas, we told you before. Jesus trusts James, John, and me the most of all the disciples. He might let you be the treasurer, since you carry the money bag now, but He would never let you be the leader next to Him," Peter insisted.

"Peter, you're really strong. You can be the bodyguard who protects Jesus. I'll be the first of His leaders," said James.

The disciples were walking behind Jesus so that He wouldn't hear them arguing. Later when they reached Peter's house, Jesus asked them, "What were you talking about as we were walking?"

No one answered. After several moments of embarrassed silence, Thomas asked, "Who will be the greatest in the kingdom of heaven?"

"Whoever wants to be the greatest must be the servant of all," Jesus said.

He called a little boy over to Him, put His arm around him, and said, "Except you become like this child, you will not see the kingdom of heaven."

"What do You mean, Jesus?" Matthew asked.

"Children love with their whole hearts. They find joy in doing kind things for others They don't worry about being the most important," Jesus answered. "I came to be a servant and give My life for many."

The disciples were quiet. Their argument was over for the moment. Other times when they thought that Jesus couldn't hear them, they argued among themselves about who would be the leaders in Jesus' new kingdom. But often, their hearts were touched by His kind deeds, His healings, His love for all, and they just wanted to be with Him and enjoy their time together.

As Jesus and the disciples made their final trip to Jerusalem, a number of women traveled with them. One of those women was the mother of James and John—or Mrs. Zebedee. One spring day among the blooming wildflowers, Mrs. Zebedee, along with her two sons, came and knelt at Jesus' feet.

"Please, Lord, give me anything I ask," she said.

"What is it that you want?" Jesus answered.

"Please, Lord, may these young men, my two sons, sit on Your right and Your left in Your new kingdom," she said.

"Can you drink the cup that I will drink?" Jesus asked, turning to James and John.

"Yes, we can. We will follow You wherever You go," they insisted.

"You don't know what you're asking. In My kingdom, the servant is the greatest of all. Besides, My Father chooses who will be on My right and on My left in My kingdom," Jesus told them.

The other disciples noticed Mrs. Zebedee and her sons kneeling at Jesus' feet. "What are they doing?" Philip asked.

"Would you look at that! Who do they think they are?" asked Thomas.

"They're trying to get ahead of us to get the most important places in Jesus' kingdom," said Judas.

The arguing started all over again. All the disciples were angry at James and John. As they continued on their journey, several of the disciples lagged behind Jesus so they could argue without His hearing them.

Once they reached Jerusalem, so many things happened that the days went flying by. Early Friday morning, James hurried to where the women were staying. He banged on the door, shouting, "It's so terrible! You'll never believe what's happening."

His mother and the other women crowded around the door. "What's happening?" someone asked. "It's Jesus! He's been arrested! Pilate has ordered that He be crucified!" James's words were difficult to understand since he was so upset.

"James, tell us again," said Mrs. Zebedee.

"Jesus will be crucified. At Calvary. With two thieves," James spoke more slowly. "Come with me. I know the place."

In two minutes, they were ready. They walked with James on the crowded streets with many other people who wanted to see the crucifixion. Some jostled each other in the effort to be first to reach the place of execution. When they arrived, the three men were already on the crosses.

"Jesus is in the middle," gasped Mrs. Zebedee. "One thief is on His right; the other is on His left."

"Why is that important, Mother?" James asked.

"Don't you remember? I asked Jesus for you and John to be on His right and on His left in His new kingdom," she explained. "And He answered, 'Can you drink the cup that I will drink?' Look at what I was asking for!"

"When I see Him, suffering for me—for all of us—I know that it will be an honor to suffer for Him some day," James said.

* * * * *

Sure enough, both brothers faithfully lived and died for Jesus. Only a few years after Jesus' death and resurrection, James was killed because of his faith in Jesus. He was killed by King Herod, the first of Jesus' disciples to die for Him. John, lived long after many of the others had died. He was active in establishing churches and wrote the fourth gospel, three letters to the churches, and the book of Revelation, a prophecy of Jesus coming to rescue His children.

OPEN YOUR BIBLE

Read the original story
Read these stories in Matthew 18:1–5; 20:20–28; and 27:55, 56. You will find the same stories in Mark 9:30–41 and 10:35–45. You can also read Luke 9:43–48.

Compare Bible stories and verses
Read John 13:1–17. What example does Jesus give of being a servant to all during the last supper He ate with His disciples?

Answer some questions
1. Why did the disciples each want to be the greatest in Christ's kingdom?
2. What were the reasons that the disciples decided to follow Jesus?
3. What radical things did the disciples learn about what Jesus' kingdom is like?

Learn a Bible verse
"Whoever wants to become great among you must be your servant, and whoever wants to be first must be slave of all. For even the Son of Man did not come to be served, but to serve, and to give his life as a ransom for many" (Mark 10:43–45).

Share Jesus with others
1. Remember a time that you served others at home, at school, in your neighborhood, or in your church. Think about how you felt when you served others. Write about your experience in your journal and talk to an adult about it.
2. Look at Matthew 27:55, 56; Mark 15:40, 41; Luke 23:49; and John 19:25–27. These verses all tell about the women who believed in Jesus and

who were at the cross. Why do you think that the names aren't exactly the same? Why is it important that Matthew, Mark, Luke, and John included in their stories the women who believed in Jesus? In your journal, make a list of the women who are important in the story of your life. Include details about why they are important.

3. Ask your pastor, teacher, or parent for the name and contact information of someone who is being God's servant. What can you do to be an encouragement to that person? Maybe you can write a letter. Maybe you can think of a way to raise some money to help with their project. Each person's situation will be different so discuss your plan with an adult and then take steps to make it happen.

Chapter 20

THE TREE CLIMBER

"Where's the crowd going?" Zacchaeus asked a passerby.

"Haven't you heard? Jesus is coming to Jericho!" the man answered.

Jesus is coming? To Jericho? I have to see Him! Zacchaeus thought as he joined the crowd. *Oh no, how will I see Him? Being short sometimes makes life difficult.* Zacchaeus remembered a short cut to the town's main street leading from the city gate to the center of town. A tall sycamore fig tree spread its lower branches right over the street. *A perfect place for a short man like me to climb the tree and get a good view of Jesus.*

Zacchaeus ran through the narrow back streets to reach the tree. Running was beneath the dignity of a man in his position as chief tax collector in the city of Jericho. Nothing mattered to Zacchaeus but seeing Jesus. Besides he was already despised because he collected taxes for the hated Roman conquerors. A little more gossip didn't matter.

He scrambled up the tree, glad for some low branches that helped him climb. He finally found the perfect branch where he'd be able to see the crowd and Jesus as they passed under the tree.

Sitting on the branch, Zacchaeus remembered going to the Jordan River to listen to John preach. John had preached baptism for the forgiveness of sins. He told his hearers to share their food and clothes with those who had none. Zacchaeus even saw some of his fellow tax collectors being baptized. John told them, "Don't collect any more money than you are required to" (see Luke 3:13). Zacchaeus longed to join them but was afraid that he might lose his position as their chief. Gradually he changed and followed John's advice, only collecting the required tax.

"Are you the Christ?" someone had asked John.

"No," John had answered. "I baptize you with water. But one who is more powerful than I will come, the straps of whose sandals I am not worthy to untie. He will baptize you with the Holy Spirit and fire" (Luke 3:16).

Zacchaeus mourned when he heard the news of John's death. Then he wanted the Messiah to arrive even more.

Zacchaeus remembered when he first heard about Jesus, he had wondered if Jesus might be the Messiah that John had predicted. He thought of the scriptures he had studied as a young man.

As he longed to meet Jesus, he made other changes. He tried to return money that he had wrongly taken.

One day he approached a rabbi whom he had overcharged. "I want to return some money to you," he said to the rabbi.

"Are you crazy? You, a tax collector, want to give me money? Hey, everyone, watch out for this man, this lover of Romans. He's trying to give me money—it must be a trick," the rabbi called to the people around him.

Zacchaeus slipped away as quickly as he could. Later, a merchant shook his head as he accepted Zacchaeus's offer.

The crowd outside the gate began shouting, "Praise God! Praise God!"

And Zacchaeus watched as blind Bartimaeus in his usual rags danced through the city gate. "Thank You, Jesus! Thank You, Jesus!" he shouted, throwing away his stick and jumping.

A crowd gathered below Zacchaeus. "Did you see it?" someone asked.

"No, tell me about it. What happened?" asked another.

"Blind Bartimaeus heard the noise of the crowd and asked what was happening. Someone said that Jesus was coming. 'Jesus, son of David, have mercy on me!' Bart shouted [Luke 18:38]. 'Sh! Be quiet!' several people called out to him. 'Son of David, have mercy on me!' [Luke 18:39], he shouted again."

"Hearing the commotion, Jesus stopped and said, 'Bring him to me.' When Bart stood beside Him, Jesus asked, 'What would you like?' 'I want to see,' Bart told Him. 'Receive your sight; your faith has healed you' [Luke 18:42], Jesus said. Then Bart could see. No wonder he is dancing for joy!"

Zacchaeus was amazed. *How often I have seen Bartimaeus by the city gate! Now he can see! Jesus is like no one else. He must be the One John the Baptist said would come.*

As the crowd neared, some people walked under the tree where Zacchaeus sat among the branches. He watched, afraid that he might miss something important. Then Jesus stopped right under the tree and looked up at Zacchaeus. His smile gave Zacchaeus hope. "Zacchaeus, come down immediately. I must stay at your house today," Jesus said (Luke 19:5).

Zacchaeus practically fell out of the tree. "Yes, yes, come to my house. Bring Your disciples. We will make a special meal for you."

"Jesus will be the guest of a sinner!" sneered some in the crowd. "He knows that is a bad thing to do. Shame on Him!"

"Jesus, I'm giving half of my property to the poor. If I have taken anyone's money falsely, I will repay him four times," Zacchaeus told Jesus.

"I don't believe that! He wouldn't have anything left," people in the crowd muttered.

But Jesus said, "Today salvation has come to this house, because this man, too, is a son of Abraham. For the Son of Man came to seek and to save the lost" (Luke 19:9, 10).

Together Jesus and Zacchaeus walked toward his house. Zacchaeus touched the shoulder of a little boy. "Do you know where I live?"

"Yes," the boy said.

"Here, take this coin, and run to my house. Please tell my wife that Jesus and His disciples will eat with us tonight."

OPEN YOUR BIBLE

Read the original story

Find the story about the healing of the blind man in Mark 10:46–52 and Luke 18:35–43. Read about Zacchaeus in Luke 19:1–10.

Compare Bible stories and verses

Read about another tax collector who chose to follow Jesus in Matthew 9:9–13; Mark 2:13–17; and Luke 5:27–32.

Answer some questions

1. How did blind Bartimaeus show his faith in Jesus?
2. Why did Zacchaeus forget about how a tax collector should act?
3. What kind of people did Jesus come to radically rescue?

Learn a Bible verse

"Jesus answered them, 'It is not the healthy who need a doctor, but the sick. I have not come to call the righteous, but sinners to repentance' " (Luke 5:31, 32).

Share Jesus with others

1. Research to see what a sycamore fig tree looks like. Draw a picture of the tree with Zacchaeus hidden in the branches and Jesus looking up to talk to him. Share your picture and tell the story of Zacchaeus.
2. Write the words to a song that Bartimaeus might sing after Jesus healed him. Read or sing your song for your family.
3. Jesus explained that His radical rescue mission was to "Seek and save the lost." He also said He had come to call "sinners to repentance." The people in the time of Jesus didn't welcome Zacchaeus to associate with them. Think

about a friend or neighbor of yours who doesn't attend church. Talk with a parent, teacher, or pastor about what kinds of church details would make your friend or neighbor feel welcome. Then invite your friend or neighbor to join you at your church. Don't be discouraged if they turn down your invitation the first few times you ask.

Part III

THE RESCUE GUARANTEED

Chapter 21

THE KING RIDES A COLT

Good morning, Zechariah, my friend!" Asher greeted his colt. "Would you like a carrot before we go walking?"

The donkey colt nuzzled Asher's coat pocket, searching for the treat. Asher chuckled. "Ah, I tricked you today. I didn't put the carrot in my pocket this morning as I usually do. I'm holding it in my hand!" Asher pulled his hand out from behind his back and opened his fingers to show Zechariah. Zechariah hungrily took the carrot and crunched it between his teeth.

"Enough crunching," interrupted Asher. "We have walking to do! Father said you are getting strong with all of the exercise I give you. After the Passover celebration, Father also said he will teach me how to train you so I can ride on your back. Then I can ride you all over the village instead of just walking with you!"

Zechariah let out a loud hee-haw in reply.

"I know," agreed Asher. "You will love taking me on rides! Maybe we will ride all the way to Jerusalem one day."

Asher led his donkey colt with a rope attached to a halter, down the dusty street, and out into the surrounding countryside. While they walked, Asher thought of the stories he had heard about the Man called Jesus. His favorite? Asher loved the story of the boy who shared his lunch. Jesus turned five barley loaves and two fish into enough food to feed at least ten thousand people. He wondered if he would have been willing to share his lunch with Jesus.

Asher's thinking was interrupted by Zechariah, who had stopped without warning to take a nibble on a few sprigs of fresh greens growing by the road.

"Keep moving, Zechariah," urged Asher. He pulled on the Zechariah's rope, but Zechariah grabbed one more bite before taking a step forward.

After an hour, Asher and Zechariah returned to their house, close to the edge of the village.

"I can see Zechariah's muscles getting as strong as iron!" Asher's father called to him from the side of the house where some men had gathered to discuss business with him. "Asher is a faithful worker," his father boasted to his friends.

Asher smiled. He liked to make his father proud of him.

"Tie Zechariah to the post in front of the house for a few minutes, and give this basket to your mother," said Asher's father.

"Okay," said Asher. He took the basket and disappeared through the door.

While Asher was inside, two men walked into the village. They walked up to Zechariah and started untying his rope. Zechariah gave a hee-haw.

Asher's father and the other men outside looked over at the sound. "Hey," shouted Asher's father. "What are you doing untying the donkey?"

Then Asher appeared in the doorway. "That's my colt," he objected.

"We are two of the disciples of Jesus. 'The Lord needs your colt, and will send it back here shortly.' "

Jesus needs Zechariah? Asher thought to himself. *I don't understand. He's just an ordinary donkey colt. But, Jesus turned that ordinary lunch into food for thousands—I wonder what He will do with my donkey.*

To the men Asher replied, "Of course! Please take him to Jesus. His name is Zechariah. Be careful though—no one has ever ridden him."

"Thank you! We'll take good care of Zechariah and return him to you before the day is over." And they led Asher's donkey away.

Just before sunset, Asher heard a familiar hee-haw. When he stepped outside of his house, he saw the two disciples leading Zechariah into the yard.

They described the events of the day to Asher. One of them reported, "It was just like the prophet Zechariah said,

"Rejoice greatly, Daughter Zion!
  Shout, Daughter Jerusalem!
See, your king comes to you,
  righteous and victorious,
lowly and riding on a donkey,
  on a colt, the foal of a donkey [Zechariah 9:9].

"Jesus rode Zechariah right into Jerusalem with people waving palm branches and shouting, 'Hosanna! Blessed is he who comes in the name of the Lord!' " added the other (Mark 11:9).

"It was the procession of a king—King Jesus!" they exclaimed together.

"My donkey carried King Jesus? I'm so happy I let Jesus borrow my colt!"

OPEN YOUR BIBLE

Read the original story

Look up this story in the Bible in Mark 11:1–11 and Luke 19:28–38.

Compare Bible stories and verses

Read about the time a boy shared his lunch with Jesus in John 6:1–15. How did Jesus bless others with the boy's gift? Why didn't Jesus let the people proclaim Him to be King after this miracle?

Answer some questions

1. What thoughts did Asher have that convinced him to let the disciples borrow his donkey colt?
2. Jesus allowed the people to greet Him like a king at this event but not at other times. What was different this time?
3. In Zechariah 9:9, the King is described as "righteous and victorious" and also as "lowly." How does this description fit with the mission of Jesus to radically rescue His people?

Learn a Bible verse

Rejoice greatly, Daughter Zion!
  Shout, Daughter Jerusalem!
See, your king comes to you,
  righteous and victorious,
lowly and riding on a donkey,
  on a colt, the foal of a donkey (Zechariah 9:9).

Share Jesus with others

1. Think about a time when someone allowed you to borrow something of theirs. Write a note to tell the person thank you. Be sure to include details about how their generosity helped you.
2. Have a discussion with your family about lending and borrowing. Ask them to share stories about times when lending or borrowing has not gone well and when it has been a blessing.
3. In your journal, write a letter to Jesus telling Him what you own that you would be willing to lend to Him. Keep a record of opportunities to share with Jesus and the details of what happened when you did.

Chapter 22

THE KING BORROWS A ROOM

"At last you have arrived for the Passover celebration, Cousin Asher!" exclaimed Ezra. "I've been wishing you were here all week long. Jesus is in Jerusalem. Everyone thinks He will soon overthrow the Romans and be the King of the Jews!"

"Ezra, wait until you hear *my* news! Jesus rode my donkey, Zechariah, when the people waved the palm branches and shouted, 'Hosanna!' Did you see him?"

"Did I see Zechariah or Jesus?"

"Both! The disciples of Jesus borrowed Zechariah. When they brought Zechariah back they told me Jesus rode him into Jerusalem!"

"I thought I recognized your donkey colt! I saw a white spot on the donkey's right front leg just like Zechariah has, but I couldn't figure out how Zechariah could be carrying Jesus. Now I understand!"

"You were there? Tell me more about it!" demanded Asher.

"Well, the news of Jesus approaching Jerusalem spread like wildfire. We heard the crowd long before they entered the city, so we rushed out to join the celebration. There was singing and shouting. People cut down palm branches and olive tree branches and waved them in front of Jesus. Many put their coats on the road so Jesus could ride over them. It was like a royal parade!"

"Did Jesus say He was the King of the Jews?"

"No, not exactly," answered Ezra. "But He didn't stop them from saying, 'Blessed is the King who comes in the name of the Lord!' And, when the Pharisees told Jesus that He should command the people to stop, Jesus answered, 'If they keep quiet, the stones will cry out' " (Luke 19:40).

"Where did the parade end?" asked Asher.

"Jesus went into the temple. Most of us followed Him. You have to remember the Passover is one of the busiest times in the temple with merchants selling animals for the offerings. Between the animal noises, the exchange of money for temple coins, and the bargaining going on it was just like a busy market day.

"Jesus looked around. He looked sad and angry all at the same time. Then

He called out, 'It is written, . . . "My house will be a house of prayer"; but you have made it "a den of robbers" ' "(Luke 19:46).

"You should have seen those merchants run! They didn't dare look Jesus in the eye. They ran as fast as an arrow flies and didn't even bother to take the animals or their money with them.

"And when it was finally quiet, Jesus told us stories—wonderful stories. One was about tenants who rented out a vineyard and wouldn't give it back to the owner. They even killed the owner's son."

"What!" exclaimed Asher.

"My favorite was about a wedding banquet for a king's son. Everyone who was invited first refused to attend the wedding! So the king invited other people who were excited to go. The king even gave them wedding clothes to wear. One man refused to put them on, and the king told his helpers to take the man away from the wedding dinner.

"Jesus said that these stories would help us understand His kingdom. I'm still trying to figure out what they mean so I can understand what the kingdom of heaven is like."

"Did He tell you stories only that first day?" asked Asher.

"No, He's been telling stories every day this week. But it's more than stories! Jesus has been healing people. Lame people now walk. Blind people can see now. Jesus healed everyone who visited Him in the temple and asked Him for help. That's why I wish you had been here all week long!"

"I've been asking Mother and Father every day to leave for Jerusalem. They said, 'The day before preparation day is soon enough to walk to your aunt and uncle's home. They will be preparing the Passover for us this year.'

"Do you think Jesus will be in the temple today?"

"I'm not sure," answered Ezra. "But wait until you hear the most exciting news yet!"

"What?"

"Guess who stopped by our house this morning?"

"Who?" asked Asher.

"Peter and John, two of the disciples of Jesus."

"Here? Why?"

"They followed my father to our house. He was carrying a water jug to help with getting ready for our meal this evening. I overheard Peter and John ask him if Jesus and His disciples could eat the Passover supper here!" exclaimed Ezra.

"What did your father say?"

"He said they were welcome to use the upstairs room. 'Anything for Jesus!' "

"Jesus borrowed my donkey. Now He is borrowing your upstairs room tonight," Asher wondered out loud.

"Some of the disciples are already here. Maybe we can offer to help them. Maybe we can see Jesus tonight!"

"Let's go ask!" said Asher. Both boys raced off to the upstairs room.

* * * * *

Asher and Ezra spent most of the afternoon helping their family and the disciples of Jesus finish preparing for the Passover supper. They cheerfully carried water, swept out rooms, and fed animals. The whole time, they looked forward to the arrival of Jesus.

At dusk, they watched a group of people climb to the upstairs room. They waved at Jesus. He smiled and waved back at them. Then He and His disciples closed the door behind them.

On the main floor of the house, Asher and Ezra joined their families for the celebration meal. They ate bitter herbs dipped in salty water to remember the difficult time the Israelites had in Egypt and their tears of despair. They drank the grape juice reminding them of the blood of the Passover lamb sprinkled on the doorposts to tell the angel to "pass over" that house. They ate the bread baked without yeast just like the people of Israel did when they had to leave Egypt on short notice and didn't have time for the bread to rise. They celebrated this anniversary of God delivering their ancestors from Egypt so miraculously, and they looked forward to the coming of the Messiah. Could it be Jesus? Each person sitting at the family table wondered the same thing.

When the meal was over, Ezra and Asher asked for permission from their fathers to go upstairs to see if Jesus and His disciples needed anything.

Upstairs, Jesus and His disciples still ate the celebration meal.

"You haven't finished the meal yet?" Ezra asked Peter.

"Well," Peter answered, "I'm embarrassed to say this, but we were having an argument about which one of us was the most important disciple. We waited and waited and waited for one of the others to wash everyone's feet. Then in the middle of the meal, Jesus stood up and took a towel. He used the water you boys brought up earlier. One by one, He washed our feet. He just finished.

"If you boys have time, stay in the corner of the room in case we need your help later."

"We have time!" Asher and Ezra answered. They quietly moved into the corner of the room by the door. They could quickly go and find anything Jesus needed from there.

Then Jesus took some of the bread. "Eat some of this bread. It is a symbol of My body that will be broken for you."

The disciples looked confused but did as Jesus asked.

Next Jesus took some of the grape juice. "Drink some of this juice. It is a symbol of My blood that will be spilled to give people a new promise of forgiveness. I won't be drinking grape juice again until we drink it together in My Father's kingdom."

Everyone drank some of the juice.

Asher and Ezra did not understand what any of this meant.

"Tonight, one of you is going to betray Me," Jesus announced.

Asher and Ezra looked at each other in horror. One of the disciples would betray Jesus? That couldn't be!

The disciples started asking questions of each other trying to figure out who would betray Jesus, and then the disciples started arguing again about who was going to be the greatest in Jesus' kingdom. Ezra and Asher wondered how they could do that so easily with Jesus sitting at the table with them.

"Friends! Stop arguing! Remember that to be the greatest you need to be a servant," said Jesus.

"Maybe that's why Jesus washed their feet," whispered Ezra to his cousin.

Next, they saw John lean over and talk to Jesus quietly. They couldn't hear any of the words, but they saw Jesus give a piece of bread to Judas. As soon as Judas had eaten the bread he stood up from the table and left the room.

"Why is he leaving?" whispered Asher.

"I think he is the one with the money bag," replied Ezra. "Maybe Jesus needs him to run an errand. But, shhhh. Jesus is talking again."

"Simon," Jesus said to Peter, "Satan wanted you, but I prayed for strength for you. When everything is over and you have repented, be sure to give your brothers strength."

"Oh, Lord, I'm ready to go to jail for You or to die for You!" answered Peter.

"Peter, tonight you will say you don't know Me three times before the rooster crows."

Asher and Ezra listened to the group as the conversation continued a few more minutes. Jesus and His disciples finished the meal and sang a hymn. Then the two boys watched everyone leave the room.

"I'm worried about Jesus!" said Asher.

"Me too," said Ezra.

"Let's start cleaning up. At least we can do something to help my mom even if we can't help Jesus."

The two boys worked in silence, buried in their own thoughts. What would tomorrow bring? They weren't sure they wanted to know.

OPEN YOUR BIBLE

Read the original story

Luke 22:7–38 is where you can read one version of the story about the last supper Jesus ate with His disciples. Look for other versions of the story in Matthew 26:17–35; Mark 14:12–31; and John 13:1–28.

Compare Bible stories and verses

Read about another meal Jesus attended where He was anointed with perfume in Matthew 26:6–16 and John 12:1–11. What is the same and what is different in the story of the Last Supper compared to the story about Jesus being anointed with perfume.

Answer some questions

1. How were the merchants in the temple changing the meaning of the Passover?
2. What did Jesus washing His disciples' feet have to do with His mission to radically rescue people from sin?
3. What do you think was the most important message Jesus wanted His disciples to hear at His last supper with them? Why?

Learn a Bible verse

"Then Jesus declared, 'I am the bread of life. Whoever comes to me will never go hungry, and whoever believes in me will never be thirsty' " (John 6:35).

Share Jesus with others

1. Work with an adult to make some bread or go to the store and buy some fancy bread. Deliver the bread and a decorated page with John 6:35 carefully written on it to someone who needs encouragement.
2. The next time you find yourself in an argument with a family member where you are trying to get your way, remember how Jesus washed the feet of His disciples. What can you do to change your part of the disagreement from, "I need to get my way," to "How can I help everyone get what they need?" Take note of the reactions of the people around you.
3. When Communion is celebrated at your church, listen carefully to the words of the pastor and compare them with the story of the Last Supper. Ask a parent, pastor, or teacher to explain any part of the Communion service you don't understand.

Chapter 23

THE KING BETRAYED

It was a familiar path. The disciples had been to the garden many times before with Jesus. However, this night was different. Everyone was quiet, but they all noticed that with every step Jesus seemed more and more weighed down with some terrible burden. They wondered, *Did Jesus really mean what He said during the Passover supper about one of us betraying Him?* Worry and fear filled theirs hearts and as they walked in the darkness.

Just inside the Gethsemane gate Jesus said, "Stay here and pray." Then to Peter, James, and John, He said, "Follow Me further into the garden."

Jesus struggled to walk on. His three disciples followed closely, grabbing His arms a couple of times to keep Him from falling. *What is happening to Jesus?* John fretted. *Tonight is so different from the time we prayed with Him on the mountain and witnessed His visit with Moses and Elijah.*

Closer to a favorite spot, Jesus said, "My soul is overwhelmed with sorrow to the point of death. . . . Stay here and keep watch" (Mark 14:34). Then He staggered deeper into the garden.

"John, I don't understand," James whispered.

The disciples wondered how this night fit in with the events of the week. A few days earlier, Jesus rode a donkey colt into Jerusalem as predicted by the prophet Zechariah. He received the praise of the people who cheered Him as their King. Yet tonight at the supper, He talked about His body broken for the disciples, His blood shed for them, and that He would be betrayed.

They glanced over at Jesus and saw Him lying flat on the ground. They heard His groans. They heard Him cry out, "Abba, Father, . . . everything is possible for you. Take this cup from me. Yet not what I will, but what you will" (Mark 14:36).

The three disciples sat in a circle and prayed. They prayed until they could no longer stay awake. Maybe because their stomachs were full from the Passover meal, maybe because it had been such a long day, or maybe it was because of the shadow of sadness in their hearts, but all three fell asleep.

"Simon, . . . are you asleep?" Jesus' voice startled them. "Couldn't you keep watch for one hour? Watch and pray so that you will not fall into temptation.

The spirit is willing, but the flesh is weak" (Mark 14:37, 38).

Startled out of his sleep, Peter looked at Jesus and then hung his head. James and John studied Jesus. His pale skin and sunken eyes worried them. Sweat dripped from His face—or was that blood? They remembered Peter's words during the Passover meal a few hours ago, "Jesus, even if everyone else deserts You, I won't."

Slowly, Jesus walked back to His prayer place. Again, the disciples saw Him facedown on the ground. They prayed until they just couldn't keep their eyes open.

I'll just rest for a minute before I pray more, John thought as he closed his eyes. But that was not a good choice. Sleep blurred the disciples' understanding of the seriousness of the moment.

"Are you asleep again?" Jesus' voice interrupted their rest.

With nothing to say, they knew they had let Jesus down a second time.

The disciples determined to stay awake as Jesus left them once more. However, after what felt like only seconds, Jesus returned to find them sleeping again. Standing tall, voice strong, He asked, "Are you still sleeping and resting? Enough! The hour has come. Look, the Son of Man is delivered into the hands of sinners. Rise! Let us go! Here comes my betrayer!" (Mark 14:41, 42).

They jumped to their feet. Betrayer? Where was the betrayer? They only saw Judas entering the garden. Oh, good! Judas had finally finished whatever his errand was when he left the Passover table and found them in the garden. They knew he would know where to look for them.

For some reason, a crowd of temple guards, temple leaders and elders, and soldiers followed Judas. Some were carrying torches. Some were carrying lanterns. Many were carrying weapons. The disciples waiting at the garden gate rushed over to stand with Jesus.

Judas walked up to Jesus and greeted Him with a kiss.

"Judas, are you betraying the Son of Man with a kiss?" Jesus asked (Luke 22:48).

Judas is betraying Jesus? John thought, *That can't be!*

Some of the men stepped toward Jesus.

"Who do you want?" Jesus asked the crowd.

"We want Jesus of Nazareth!" they called out.

"I am he," Jesus answered (John 18:5).

When Jesus said those words, the crowd was knocked to the ground like a strong wind blew them all down at the same time. When they recovered, they again rushed toward Jesus.

"Who do you want?" Jesus asked again.

"We want Jesus of Nazareth!" they demanded.

"I told you that I am he. If you are looking for me, then let these men go" (John 18:8).

Peter was prepared. He pulled out his sword and started swinging, but his aim wasn't too good. After all, a fisherman isn't trained to use a sword like a soldier. However, he managed to slice off the ear of Malchus, the high priest's servant.

Jesus stopped everything. "Put your sword away! Shall I not drink the cup the Father has given me?" (John 18:11).

The cup? The disciples had heard Him pray about a cup. He asked the Father to take it away, if possible. The confusion began to clear as they realized everything was about to change.

The soldiers arrested Jesus. They tried to grab the rest of the disciples, but they all ran—just like Jesus said. *Oh, why didn't we stay awake and pray?* Each man wondered.

John ran until his muscles burned and he needed air. When he heard footsteps from behind he tensed, ready to run again, but then Peter called his name.

"John! Wait for me!" Peter gasped.

"Where are the others?" John called back to him.

"I don't know. Everyone scattered trying to get away from the soldiers."

"Do you think we are safe?" John asked when Peter stood next to him trying to catch his breath.

"None of the soldiers followed us," Peter replied.

"Where are they taking Jesus?"

"Those were soldiers sent by the high priest. My guess is they are taking Him to Caiaphas," Peter suggested.

"Let's go!" John said. "Jesus needs us. Maybe we can catch up to the soldiers."

Peter hesitated, then he turned around and started running with John toward the soldiers instead of away from them. They figured they could follow at a safe distance and be able to at least see where Jesus was taken.

A full moon lit their path as they ran back down the Mount of Olives, across the Kidron Valley, and toward the east wall of Jerusalem. They watched as a group led Jesus through the city gate and then followed them to the high priest's palace.

Because the high priest knew him, John was allowed to go inside with Jesus. He moved as close as possible to where Jesus stood so he could hear and see everything.

John clenched his fists as he watched Jesus being tied up like an animal and pushed around by the soldiers. Why were they treating Him like this? Then he saw Annas waiting at the door of his house, ready to come outside. He was the father-in-law of the high priest, Caiaphas. If Annas was in charge, things looked grim for Jesus. He had a well-known reputation for twisting justice.

Then John remembered that Peter stood waiting outside, so while the temple leaders scrambled to get everything set up for Annas, he went back to the courtyard door and spoke to one of the servant girls, "May my friend also come inside?"

She agreed to open the door for Peter, but she looked at him closely as he walked in. "Hey! Aren't you one of Jesus' disciples too?"

Peter must have been afraid because he answered, "No, I'm not!"

Peter moved closer to the fire to get warm, while John headed back to Jesus.

Jesus stood in front of Annas. He was saying, "I have spoken openly to the world, . . . I always taught in synagogues or at the temple, where all the Jews come together. I said nothing in secret. Why question me? Ask those who heard me. Surely they know what I said" (John 18:20–21).

Annas must have accused Jesus of trying to lead a secret rebellion!

An official near Jesus slapped Him in the face. "Is this the way you answer the high priest?" (John 18:22).

Jesus answered him, "If I said something wrong, . . . testify as to what is wrong. But if I spoke the truth, why did you strike me?" (John 18:23).

"Take him to Caiaphas!" Annas commanded.

God in Heaven, help Jesus! John prayed.

Caiaphas waited for Jesus. He was surrounded by a big group of temple elders and teachers of the law. A large number of "witnesses" waited nearby.

When Jesus arrived, Caiaphas called on men to testify against Jesus, looking for enough evidence to condemn Him. Jewish law required that two witnesses tell the same story before a man can be convicted of a crime. Even though witnesses told stories for over an hour, not once did two men tell matching stories—until a couple of ruffians announced, "Jesus said He could destroy God's temple and then build it again in only three days."

Caiaphas's evil grin widened, "Well, do You have an answer for what these men are accusing You of doing?"

Jesus said nothing.

Frustrated and angry, Caiaphas raised his voice and commanded Jesus, "I charge You under oath by the Living God: Tell us if You are the Christ, the Son of God."

Jesus had to answer that, and He clearly replied, "Yes, it is as you say. But I say to all of you: In the future you will see the Son of Man sitting at the right hand of the Mighty One and coming on the clouds of heaven."

Unmeasured furor was unleashed at that moment. Angry Caiaphas tore his priestly robes in horror and exclaimed, "What more evidence do we need to convict the man? With His own words He claims to be equal with God." And to the temple leaders he asked, "What do you think?"

"He deserves to die!"

The crowd rushed toward Jesus. Some spit on Him. Some punched Him with their fists. Others blindfolded Him, slapped Him, and then demanded that He prophesy to tell who it was that hit Him. Never had John seen men treat another so badly. His heart ached. Jesus deserved none of that.

Jesus said nothing.

John couldn't bear to watch so he turned away from Jesus and moved closer to Peter. Every hateful blow to Jesus made Peter cringe. Those around him at the fire noticed his reaction. "This man belongs to the group that follows Jesus," accused one of the servant girls.

Peter replied, "I don't know what you are talking about."

"Wait a minute! You are part of them!" said another. "Didn't I see you with him in the garden?" (John 18:26).

"I don't know this Man!" exclaimed Peter.

One second later, a rooster crowed. Peter looked at Jesus, then ran out of the courtyard door, weeping bitterly.

By the time the darkness of night gave way to morning, the soldiers were leading Jesus to Pilate, the Roman governor. This night to forget was finally over, but the most terrible day of all was about to begin.

OPEN YOUR BIBLE

Read the original story

Read the story about how Jesus was arrested and put on trial in Matthew 26:36–75; Mark 14:32–72; Luke 22:39–65; and John 18:1–27.

Compare Bible stories and verses

Compare the details from this story to Jesus' prediction that Judas would betray Him and Peter would deny Him as told in Mark 14:27–31 and John 13:18–38.

Answer some questions

1. What did Peter, James, and John learn about Jesus in the garden?
2. Why do you think Jesus was silent when He was asked questions by the high priest?
3. What radical claims did Jesus make when Caiaphas commanded Him to tell under oath if He was the Son of God?

Learn a Bible verse

Right before He was arrested Jesus gave His disciples a promise in John 14:1–3. Spend time memorizing these verses: "Do not let your hearts be troubled. You believe in God; believe also in me. My Father's house has many rooms; if that were not so, would I have told you that I am going there to prepare a place for you? And if I go and prepare a place for you, I will come back and take you to be with me that you also may be where I am."

Share Jesus with others

1. Create a set of pictures to tell the major events of this story. Add the words each of the people in your pictures would have said to make the story telling more complete. Share your pictures to tell the story of Jesus' betrayal and trial with the high priest.
2. Pretend you are Peter. Write what you think Peter would have written to tell his version of the story on the night Jesus was arrested in the Garden of Gethsemane.
3. Practice a monologue performance (one person acting out a story) based on what you created for activity 2. Share your monologue with an audience.

Chapter 24

THE KING CRUCIFIED

He claims to be the Son of God! That makes Him a blasphemer! He must die!" screamed the high priest.

"No, don't do this!" John wanted to cry out. "Jesus is the Messiah!" However, out of fear for his own safety, John did not dare say a word when the temple leaders reached their early-morning decision. Only Roman law prevented the angry group from killing Jesus right then and there. Pilate, the Roman governor, must make the final ruling to put Jesus to death.

John followed behind at a guarded distance as Jesus' captors dragged Him to Pilate's palace. Not knowing where Peter went after the rooster crowed, John had no way to communicate with him. But surely some of the other disciples were anxious to hear more about Jesus, so John kept watch for them along the way.

Once at the palace, the Jews refused to go inside Pilate's house because they wanted to stay ceremonially clean for the Passover. Instead, they sent a message to him. Pilate arrived with a scowl on his face, probably caused by the request for his judgment so early in the morning.

"What do you want?" Pilate asked Caiaphas. "What has this Man done?"

"He's a criminal. We wouldn't have brought Him to you if He wasn't."

"Then deal with it yourself. Judge Him by your own laws. Don't bring Him to me."

"We don't have the power to execute Him," objected Caiaphas, the high priest. "This Man causes rebellion and unrest all over our country. He tells people to not pay their taxes to Caesar and claims to be a king."

False evidence is their only hope of having Jesus executed, John thought as he listened. *The Romans do not like it when someone tries to rise to political power.*

"Alright, alright. I'll talk with the prisoner," agreed Pilate.

* * * * *

"John! John!" James called to his brother after Jesus was taken inside Pilate's judgment hall.

"James! Where are the others?"

"I don't know. But I had to find you. When you didn't return last night to the room where we celebrated the Passover I figured you followed Jesus. I met some people on the street this morning who reported that Jesus was being taken to Pilate's palace."

"James, it was so awful! Caiaphas asked Jesus if He is God's Son. When He said yes, the temple leaders cried, 'Blasphemy!' They've asked Pilate to execute Him!"

"Where is Jesus now?"

"Inside, with Pilate."

"Will Pilate go along with their plan?" asked James.

"I pray not. Look! Pilate is bringing Jesus back outside. Let's listen to what he tells Caiaphas."

"There's no reason for you to bring this Man to me. He hasn't done anything wrong."

"Governor, you don't understand. His teachings have been upsetting people from Galilee all the way to Jerusalem," claimed Caiaphas.

"Did you say Galilee? Well, in that case, I will send Jesus to King Herod. The ruler of Galilee should have a chance to pass judgment on a troublemaker from his own region. Herod happens to be visiting Jerusalem."

To the soldiers Pilate ordered, "Take Jesus to Herod!"

"Now what do we do?" asked James.

"We follow the crowd to Herod. We won't be able to go inside, but we must follow Jesus!"

* * * * *

The soldiers rudely pushed Jesus into the courtyard of Herod's palace. James and John found a safe corner to wait. The two brothers paced back and forth, wringing their hands, and hoping God would rescue Jesus.

A while later, soldiers surrounded Jesus when He walked out of Herod's palace, almost as if they were protecting Him from the angry, jeering crowd. James and John felt heartsick. Jesus wore the purple robe of a king but the crowd taunted and made fun of Him as if He were a fool. Jesus said nothing in return.

The swollen river of people followed Jesus back to Pilate's palace. They listened to the repeated early morning accusations from Caiaphas and the other temple leaders. They also heard Pilate's reply.

"Look," said Pilate, "I've already told you this Man is innocent. Apparently, Herod agrees with me. But, to make you happy, I will punish Him and then set Him free."

"No! Take Him away!" screamed the mob of angry Jews.

"The Passover custom is that I release a prisoner to you. Do you want me to release Jesus or Barabbas?"

"Barabbas! Give us Barabbas!"

"How can they ask for Barabbas?" John wondered out loud.

"Isn't he the one who committed murder trying to lead a rebellion against Rome?" added James.

"Jesus! Give us Jesus!" James and John tried to yell but their voices were swallowed by the roar of the others.

"John, look at Pilate. He's reading a note."

"He has a strange look on his face. I wonder what the note says."

"Soldiers, take Jesus away and punish Him." Pilate commanded.

Ugly sounds echoed from behind the wall where the soldiers took Jesus. A whip cracked more times than James and John wanted to count. Skin slapping skin followed "Hail, King of the Jews!" echoed in rough voices. When it finally stopped, the soldiers pulled Jesus back to Pilate. Bruises covered His face. He wore the blood-soaked royal robe and, on His head, sat a crown fashioned from the branches of a thorny bush. Blood ran from His wounds.

"I can't look!" cried James.

"Pray!" replied John. "Maybe Pilate will be able to set Jesus free now."

"Jesus has been punished, but there's no reason to put Him to death," Pilate stated.

"Crucify Him! Crucify Him!" chanted the crowd led by the temple leaders.

"Why?" asked Pilate. "You can crucify Him if you want to but I don't think He has done anything wrong!"

"We have a law, and according to that law he must die, because he claimed to be the Son of God" (John 19:7).

"Pilate is taking Jesus back inside! Do you think that's a good sign?" asked John.

"Did you see his face go pale when the priests told him Jesus claimed to be God's Son?"

Pilate returned to the crowd after a short time and stated, "There's no reason to execute Jesus!"

"If you set Him free then you are not Caesar's friend."

After that, Pilate called for a bowl of water. He dipped his hands into the bowl and called out to the crowd, "I am innocent of this Man's blood. It is your responsibility!"

"Let His blood be on us and on our children!" the crowd cried.

"Here is your King!" said Pilate.

"We have no king but Caesar," the chief priests answered (John 19:15).

"Crucify Him! Crucify Him!" the frenzied mob began again.

"The crowd won't listen to reason," said James.

"Jesus is doomed to die!" cried John.

"Take Him then. You crucify Him," declared Pilate. "Barabbas is released to you instead."

* * * * *

Word that Jesus was to be crucified quickly spread throughout the city. People poured from their homes into the streets. Many of the disciples and several of the women who followed Jesus also joined the throng that filled the path to Golgotha, the name of the hill outside of Jerusalem where criminals were executed.

The soldiers had placed the cross intended for Barabbas on the shoulders of Jesus. He stumbled and fell under the burden. When they realized Jesus would not be able to carry the cross all the way to Golgotha, the soldiers grabbed a man from the crowd and forced him to carry the cross for Jesus.

Up ahead, John spotted Mary, the mother of Jesus, closer to Jesus than James and himself. She and the other women were crying out in despair and sympathy. They didn't care what the priests or the mob thought.

Jesus turned to them and said, "Don't weep for Me; weep for yourselves and for your children."

Eventually, James and John caught up to the women.

The process of Jesus being placed on the cross was horrible and grisly. Jesus was hung in between two men—two thieves. Pilate ordered a sign made for the top of the cross and had it written in three languages so everyone present for the Passover could read it. It said, "JESUS OF NAZARETH, THE KING OF THE JEWS" (see John 19:19).

"John, did you hear that temple leader over there complaining?" James asked.

"No. What is he saying?"

"Apparently they tried to have Pilate change the sign to 'This man claimed to be king of the Jews' but Pilate wouldn't make the change" (see John 19:21).

They watched the soldiers rolling dice for Jesus' clothes, and they watched as Jesus suffered in silence. As they watched their Master dying, their hopes of Him being the Messiah were dying with Him.

Yet even while Jesus suffered, He thought of others. Shortly before the end, Jesus looked down from the cross and saw His mother, Mary. He said to her, "Dear woman, here is your son" and to John, "Here is your mother." Understanding His request, John took the responsibility of caring for Mary.

"I thirst," Jesus called. Someone offered Him a sponge soaked in wine vinegar. Jesus took a few sips, then cried out, "It is finished" and took one final breath.

Mary sobbed deeply, grieving as if a piece of her soul died with Him.

James and John decided to take her away from the gloomy and sorrowful site, and they half carried her to the borrowed upper room. Surely the family would understand their need to borrow the room a while longer. There they found all of the other disciples—except the traitor, Judas.

Later they learned that the priests requested that the legs of the criminals be broken to shorten the death process. However, Jesus was already dead as proved by the blood and water that poured from a wound from a soldier's sword, so they didn't break His legs. Clearly, the priests didn't want the Golgotha scene to ruin the Passover.

Joseph of Arimathea went to Pilate and requested permission to take the body of Jesus. He and Nicodemus prepared Jesus' body with burial spices—seventy-five pounds of myrrh and aloes. These two members of the Sanhedrin were afraid of the temple leaders while Jesus was alive, but now they openly proved they were His followers. Joseph buried Jesus in the tomb he had been preparing for himself in a garden not too far from Golgotha.

While the sun set, the disciples huddled in the upper room in silence. The most terrible day finally ended. The Sabbath rest began, but no rest was to be found in their hearts.

OPEN YOUR BIBLE

Read the original story

Find John's story of Jesus being crucified in John 18:28–19:42.

Compare Bible stories and verses

Compare John's version of the crucifixion of Jesus with the stories by the other writers of the Gospels. Find them in Matthew 27:11–66; Mark 15; and Luke 23. Why do you think there are differences?

Answer some questions

1. Pilate believed Jesus had done nothing worthy of death. Why do you think it was so difficult for Pilate to release Jesus?
2. Why do you think Pilate refused to change the sign he had made from "King of the Jews" to "this man claimed to be king of the Jews"?
3. When Jesus died on the cross, it appeared that His mission had ended in

failure and Satan had won. In reality, how is His death the foundation of His work to radically rescue people from sin?

Learn a Bible verse

"You see, at just the right time, when we were still powerless, Christ died for the ungodly. Very rarely will anyone die for a righteous person, though for a good person someone might possibly dare to die. But God demonstrates his own love for us in this: While we were still sinners, Christ died for us" (Romans 5:6–8).

Share Jesus with others

1. Has there ever been a time when a "crowd" of people encouraged you to make a decision you didn't want to make? Compare your story with Pilate's story. Write the similarities in your journal. Think about a plan for what you will do the next time you are in the same situation. Write the plan details in your journal. Pray for strength to carry out your plan.
2. Luke 23:34 records that while Jesus hung on the cross, He asked His Father to forgive the people who were crucifying Him. Think about someone who is making life difficult for you. Choose to pray for the person every day for a month. You might be surprised at what happens. Share the story with a parent.
3. Read Isaiah 53 to find verses that prophesied about Jesus. Plan a Scripture reading to share at church or at school that starts with a verse or two from Isaiah 53 followed by verses from one of the four versions of the crucifixion in Matthew, Mark, Luke, or John that give evidence the prophecy was fulfilled by Jesus. Read another passage from Isaiah 53 followed by more verses from the Gospels. Repeat this process for several of the prophecies in Isaiah. End the Scripture reading with Romans 5:6–8. Recruit friends to practice and share the verses with an audience. Consider adding costumes to your presentation.

Chapter 25

THE KING RESURRECTED

Peter! John! Wake up!" Mary Magdalene urged frantically, pushing through the door.

"What's wrong?" John mumbled, half asleep. Dawn still waited to make its appearance.

"The body of Jesus is gone!" She started to cry.

Peter sat straight up from the floor in his corner of the borrowed upstairs room. "What? How can that be?"

"I don't know," Mary answered tearfully. "But it's gone! Someone has taken the body of Jesus out of the tomb and we don't know where He is!"

"Calm down and give us more details," John suggested.

"This morning I couldn't sleep. Even though it was dark, I decided to go to the garden and visit the tomb of Jesus. I just wanted to be close to Him. I know that might sound silly, but I thought I could pray—and cry. I also wanted to help the other women finish wrapping His body for burial."

"How were you going to roll away the big stone in front of the tomb?" Peter asked.

"We figured we'd ask the gardener. But it doesn't matter! It was already rolled away and His body is gone!" Mary began weeping again.

Peter looked at John with wide eyes, pushed his blanket away, and charged for the door. John followed, two steps behind. When they reached the street in front of the house John darted off and easily beat Peter to the tomb.

Out of breath, John stood at the entrance. Just as Mary reported, the stone was rolled away. He looked inside and saw the linen burial strips, but he wasn't sure if he should go in or not.

Then Peter raced up and didn't stop; he rushed right into the cave-like grave and gazed at the strips of cloth that had been wrapped around Jesus. "John, look. Here's the cloth that was around Jesus' face. Get in here! You've got to see for yourself. Jesus is gone!"

Once inside, John asked, "Peter, is it possible that Jesus is alive? We need to go back and tell the others what we've seen! Now!"

As they ran back to their friends, a seed of hope sprouted in John's heart.

Mary was missing when they reached the other disciples. "She decided to return to Jesus' tomb shortly after you left," they shared.

Just as they started to describe the rolled-away stone, the grave clothes, and the empty tomb, Mary burst into the room.

"He's alive! I've seen Him! He talked to me," she gasped between breaths.

"You talked with Jesus?" John asked.

"Yes, John! I talked with Jesus!"

"What did He say?" the other disciples begged in unison.

"I walked back to the tomb to have another look. While I cried, two angels surprised me. Their clothes were pure white and they sat where Jesus' body used to be. They talked to me. 'Woman, why are you crying?'

"I told them the same thing I told you earlier. I turned around and through my tears, I saw a Man I thought might be the gardener. He also asked me a question. 'Woman, why are you crying? Who is it you are looking for?'

" 'Please tell me where the body of Jesus is. I'll go get Him,' I sobbed.

" 'Mary,' He said. He called me by name! As soon as I heard Him say my name, I recognized His voice.

" 'Teacher!' I exclaimed. I rushed forward to hug Him, but He stopped me.

" 'Do not hold on to me, for I have not yet ascended to the Father. Go instead to my brothers and tell them, "I am ascending to my Father and your Father, to my God and your God" ' [John 20:17].

"Jesus is alive! I've seen Him! I've talked to Him and He talked to me!" Mary finished her story excitedly.

Mary's words watered the growing hope.

However, the disciples still feared for their lives. They'd seen what had been done to Jesus, so they didn't dare let down their guard.

"It will be safer if we lock the door and stay inside for a few days," Peter suggested.

They all agreed.

That evening, while everyone sat around the table where they had shared the Passover meal, Jesus unexpectedly appeared. "Peace be with you!" (John 20:19).

The disciples stared at Him in silence. How did He get through the locked door?

He showed them His hands. He showed them His feet. He showed them where the soldier's spear pierced Him. "Peace be with you! As the Father has sent me, I am sending you. . . . Receive the Holy Spirit" (John 20:21, 22).

* * * * *

After Jesus died, the disciples couldn't imagine that He would be resurrected. But three days later, they discovered that Jesus truly is alive! They saw Him with their own eyes. They talked with Him. They ate food with Him.

Jesus' mission to radically rescue people from sin and Satan was accomplished, and now the Light of the World is preparing a place in heaven for His children. And, He's coming back soon to take them home.

Eventually, John wrote a record of Jesus' life. But he admitted that "Jesus did many other things as well. If every one of them were written down, I suppose that even the whole world would not have room for the books that would be written" (John 21:25). For the rest of his life, John urged people to believe in Jesus—the One who created our world and everything in it and the One who gave His life to cover all our sins.

Jesus wants to give you peace and hope for a forever life with Him. Choose to be His follower today.

OPEN YOUR BIBLE

Read the original story

Find the story of Jesus' resurrection in Matthew 28; Mark 16; Luke 24; and John 20.

Compare Bible stories and verses

During the time of Paul, in a city called Corinth, there were people who began to wonder if Jesus had really been raised from the dead. Read 1 Corinthians 15:1–10 to find out how Paul answered them. How is Paul's answer convincing?

Answer some questions

1. What radical event happened on Sunday morning that proved Jesus has the power to rescue His followers?
2. Who did Jesus talk to after He was resurrected?
3. From your reading of this story in the Bible, describe how various people reacted when they heard the news of the Resurrection.

Learn a Bible verse

In 1 Thessalonians 4:16–18 Jesus makes a promise about how He will radically rescue His people when He returns—people who have died believing in Him and people who are alive and waiting for His return: "For the Lord himself will come down from heaven, with a loud command, with the voice of the archangel and with the trumpet call of God, and the dead in Christ will rise first. After that, we who are still alive and are left will be caught up together with them in the clouds to meet the Lord in the air. And so we will be with the Lord forever. Therefore encourage one another with these words."

Share Jesus with others

1. Find and listen to a song about the crucifixion and resurrection of Jesus. Share the song and what it means to you with a friend.
2. Jesus predicted His death and resurrection but the disciples didn't understand. Think about a time when someone told you about a future event but you didn't understand. Write your story in your journal.
3. Plan an Easter activity for your family that focuses on the Resurrection story. Write verses from the story on slips of paper, and hide them in safe places. When everyone is together, tell your family to race to find the slips of paper. After all of them have been found, work together to put the verses in the correct order to tell the story. Work with a parent to plan a family celebration to thank Jesus for His radical rescue.

Chapter 26

THE KING'S PROMISE

"Come for a walk with Me," Jesus said to the disciples. They were back in Jerusalem after Jesus had met with a larger group of His followers on a mountainside in Galilee. Jesus had told His followers to tell people about Him so that they could also become His friends.

The disciples followed Jesus from the upper room where they had been staying since the Last Supper. Many of the people in the street noticed them walking along with Jesus as they had done so many times before.

"Look there are Jesus and His disciples! They look so happy. Seeing them together makes me feel like everything is right again," some women commented.

"Isn't that Jesus and His disciples?" the group overheard a man ask his companion.

"How can that be? Jesus was killed by the Romans a number of weeks ago," his friend answered. "He was crucified outside the city gate. I saw Him on the cross."

"I did too. The priests said that those men, His disciples, stole His body so people would think that He was resurrected as He said He would be," said the first man.

"That's no dead body. He's alive! The Resurrection story must be true! Have you ever heard of such a thing?" asked the second man.

"Well, yes, I have. Don't you remember how Jesus raised Lazarus of Bethany a few months ago?" the first man reminded his friend.

"Of course, you're right. We have seen and heard miracles these last few years. Some people think Jesus is the promised Messiah written about in the Scriptures."

Jesus and the disciples walked on and didn't hear the rest of the conversation. "Where are we going?" the disciples asked each other.

"This is the way to the Garden of Gethsemane," said Peter. "Maybe that is where Jesus wants to take us." All the disciples remembered Jesus praying in the garden before His trials. They remembered how they had all fallen asleep while Jesus prayed alone.

"If we had prayed without falling asleep that night, we might not have run away when the men came to arrest Him," said James. They all nodded.

But Jesus didn't stop at the Garden of Gethsemane. He kept on walking.

"Jesus, where are we going?" Philip asked.

"You'll see," He answered.

They walked in the direction of Bethany. "Maybe Jesus wants to visit Mary, Martha, and Lazarus. Seeing them again would be great," someone said.

But Jesus turned onto another path that went away from their house. Soon they came to the top of the Mount of Olives. The disciples gazed at the temple and the city of Jerusalem below them. Memories of all the times they had spent with Jesus in that city flooded their minds.

Standing on the top of the mountain, they crowded around Jesus. "Is this the time you're going to restore the kingdom of Israel?" Thomas asked.

"The Father will do that in His time and with His own authority," Jesus answered. "Remember what I told you before. Stay in Jerusalem and pray. God will send His promised Spirit to be with you and prepare you for the great task I'm giving to you. After Jerusalem, go to the rest of Judaea and Samaria. Then I will send you to all the world so that many may learn about Me and be saved."

"Jesus, do You mean that Your kingdom is about more than freeing us from the Romans? It isn't a kingdom here on earth with a throne and a crown? You wore a crown of thorns to free us from sin," Thomas said.

"Yes, Thomas, My kingdom is about people following God. Some day when I come back, it will be a kingdom with a throne and a crown too," Jesus assured him. "But that kingdom will never end."

"Jesus, remember when You sent us out two by two to heal and preach," Nathanael asked. "Were You preparing us for this new task of going everywhere to preach about You?"

"Ah, Nathanael, you're absolutely right," Jesus said.

Then Jesus rose in the air and disappeared into a cloud. The disciples were shocked. They called out to Jesus.

"Jesus, don't leave us."

"We need You."

"Please stay here with us longer."

"We won't know what to do without You."

"Jesus, please come back."

"Can't He stay with us always?"

They remembered Jesus' promise, "And I am with you always, to the very end of the age" (see Matthew 28:20).

The disciples, staring up into the sky, longed to get just one more glimpse of their Lord. While they were still looking for Jesus, two men dressed in white stood beside them. "You men from Galilee, why are you staring up into the sky? Jesus who just left you has gone to heaven to be with His Father. Someday He will come back in the same way you just saw Him go into heaven." Then the two men disappeared.

"Jesus is really gone?" questioned James.

"Yes, Jesus is really gone. What shall we do?" asked John.

"Don't you remember?" Peter asked. "He said that He was going away and we couldn't go with Him."

"Yes, He also promised that He would prepare a place for us and come back to get us so that we could be with Him," Philip added.

"He did say that shortly before we went to the garden. What did He tell us to do?" asked Andrew.

"He said that we should wait in Jerusalem until He sends us the Holy Spirit," answered Thomas.

"Jerusalem, but where should we go in Jerusalem?" asked Peter.

"Let's go back to the upper room where we've been staying since the night Jesus was arrested," John suggested.

The men walked back down the mountain, again remembering all the times and places they had been with Jesus. Matthew started singing a passage from Psalm 24, "Lift up your heads, you gates."

Some of the others joined in. "Be lifted up, you ancient doors, that the King of glory may come in."

The rest sang the response. "Who is this King of glory?"

The first group sang,

> "The LORD strong and mighty,
> the LORD mighty in battle.
> Lift up your heads, you gates;
> lift them up, you ancient doors,
> that the King of glory may come in."

"Who is this King of glory?" sang the second group.

"The LORD almighty—he is the King of glory," they all sang together.

"I can just imagine the angels singing that psalm as Jesus enters the gates of heaven today," Matthew said, and the rest agreed.

"How long do you think it took Him to get to heaven?" asked Peter. "Do you think that He's already there?"

"I guess we don't know," said John. "Maybe He's already there."

They sang some more psalms as they neared the gates of Jerusalem. The two men they had heard talking as they left with Jesus called to them, "Hey, where is Jesus? He was with you when you left here a couple of hours ago," the first man said.

"Yeah, where is He?" the second one asked.

"He's gone. He rose up into a cloud. Two men dressed in white said that He will come back someday. Then they were gone too," all of the disciples told part of the story.

"But you don't look sad and depressed. Why aren't you crying?" the first man asked.

"Yes, we're happy. We're even joyful. All of this is part of God's plan to save everyone who believes in Him," again they all talked at once. "Why don't you join us in following Jesus? He promised to be with us always and to come back to take us to be with Him. That can include you too."

"We were talking about following Jesus earlier when we saw you walking with Him," the second man added. "Now that He's gone, we'll have to pray about it some more."

As the disciples walked up the steps to the upper room, John asked the others, "Do you remember when Jesus said this, 'And I, when I am lifted up from the earth, will draw all people to myself' [see John 12:32]? Did He mean when He was lifted up on the cross or when He was lifted up to heaven?"

"Maybe He meant both," said Peter. "Already, I see many people turning to Jesus."

"When He sends us the Holy Spirit as He promised, we will see many, many people believe in Jesus."

Together they knelt in prayer. Each one added to the prayer. "Dear Father, Yes, we miss Jesus, but we trust You to send the Holy Spirit, the Comforter just as Jesus promised. We know that many will believe in Jesus. Now we wait patiently for what You will do, knowing that someday we will be reunited with You. In the name of Jesus, Amen."

OPEN YOUR BIBLE

Read the original story

Read the Scripture passages about Jesus going back to heaven in Matthew 28:16–20; Mark 16:15–20; Luke 24:45–53; and Acts 1:1–11.

Compare Bible stories and verses

Read Genesis 5:21–23 and Hebrews 11:5, 6 to find the story of Enoch, a man God took to heaven. Compare this story with the story of Jesus going back to heaven.

Answer some questions

1. What promise did the angels make to the disciples as they looked at Jesus going up in the air?
2. What did the disciples understand about the mission of Jesus to radically rescue His people when He returned to heaven?
3. Why weren't the disciples sad when Jesus left?

Learn a Bible verse

Memorize this promise about Jesus returning to finish His work of radically rescuing His people: " 'Men of Galilee,' they said, 'why do you stand here looking into the sky? This same Jesus, who has been taken from you into heaven, will come back in the same way you have seen him go into heaven' " (Acts 1:11).

Share Jesus with others

1. Write a joyful song like one the angels might have sung when Jesus went back to heaven. Sing your song for your family.
2. Write an imaginary conversation between two angels welcoming Jesus back to heaven. What do they say to each other about the radical rescue plan that is guaranteed by the death and resurrection of Jesus? What do they say to Jesus when they talk to Him? Ask a family member to help you read the conversation out loud.
3. Think about a time in your life when you had to say goodbye to a friend or relative who was going away but promised to see you again. It's been about two thousand years since Jesus went back to heaven. Sometimes people wonder why He's taking so long to keep His promise to return and finish the radical rescue. Read 2 Peter 3:8, 9. According to these verses, why has so much time passed? Share your thoughts and questions with a parent, teacher, or pastor.

MY FAVORITE BIBLE VERSES I HAVE LEARNED

WAYS I HAVE BEEN ABLE TO SHARE JESUS WITH OTHERS